The Orphan

The Orphan

A JOURNEY TO WHOLENESS

Audrey Punnett

The Orphan
A Journey to Wholeness
Copyright © 2014 by Audrey Punnett
First Edition
ISBN 978-1-77169-016-4 Paperback
ISBN 978-1-77169-017-1 eBook

Published simultaneously in Canada, the United Kingdom, and the United States of America by Fisher King Press. For information on obtaining permission for use of material from this work, submit a written request to:

permissions@fisherkingpress.com

Fisher King Press
www.fisherkingpress.com
+1-831-238-7799

Many thanks to all who have directly or indirectly provided permission to quote their works. Every effort has been made to trace all copyright holders; however, if any have been overlooked, the author will be pleased to make the necessary arrangements at the first opportunity. See page 151 for a list of contributing individuals and organizations.

The front cover image, *Solo* © is from an original painting by Susan Bostrom-Wong
www.susanbostromwong.com

DEDICATION

Even though they are gone they will always remain with me.

My parents, Louis and Marjorie Punnett,
who instilled curiosity, patience and perseverance

My analytic parents, Mario Jacoby in kinship
and Florence Grossenbacher who intuited my
journey to Zurich

ACKNOWLEDGEMENTS

For me the orphan journey began in Switzerland. Sometimes one seems to have to go to a foreign country or space for wisdom, and through many synchronicities several doors opened for me to explore this path.

When one is on the journey opportunities arise if we are open to them. While in Switzerland in order to survive financially, I did many menial tasks and one of them was dog sitting. That was how I met Susan and Chris Joenck; while at their home looking through their magazines, I discovered the picture libraries in England which opened up a world of visual images of the orphan about which I would later write. Many of the images in this book come from the Bridgeman Art Library and the Hulton Getty Picture Archives in London that these archives introduced to me.

While in Switzerland Ellie Stillman, an American who worked in the library at the C.G. Jung Institute in Küsnacht, introduced me to members of the international community who became my friends, colleagues and supporters, which was a very important synchronicity. In addition, the staff at the C.G. Jung Institute, Elena Eckels, Lotti Egli, Irene Fueter, John Granrose, Helga Kopecky, and Frances Stadler supported me in many immeasurable ways. All of you helped to give me a sense of home.

I especially want to express my appreciation to the analysands who gave me permission to include vignettes of our clinical interactions and dream material. Personal specifics were altered to make them unidentifiable. What you have shared has given the orphan a face with your personal stories.

My heartfelt thanks goes to those Jungian groups who invited me to talk about this subject: the Hokianga Jung Group of New Zealand; the Analytical Psychology Club of San Francisco; the C.G. Jung Society, Victoria, British Columbia, Canada; the C.G. Jung Society, Halifax, Nova Scotia, Canada; the Jungian Dream Group, O'Regan's, Newfoundland, Canada; the SandPlay Association of Taiwan and the Taiwan Union Conference, Taipei, Taiwan. The questions and interactions from these groups highlighted for me the engagement and power of an archetypal connection.

For those who read through the manuscript, I am most grateful for your comments and questions: Andreas Schweizer, who kept me focused on the meaning of the archetype and who understood this journey; Sue Kuba, whose support and encouragement was always present; and Josephine Evetts-Secker, whose lectures on this subject were inspiring and who first encouraged me to write more on this theme. Kathrin Asper guided this research over many years and John Hill lent his knowledge about the journey of finding a home within oneself. While Mario Jacoby, my analyst, did not live to see this publication, he read through the manuscript, walked with me on this journey and changed my life.

My appreciation is also extended to Susan Bostrom-Wong for generously contributing the cover image *Solo* – her art is truly inspired. Lastly, my gratitude is extended to Mel Mathews, publisher of Fisher King Press, who epitomizes what it means to surrender to psyche's plan. Our synchronistic crossing of paths led to this publication.

Audrey Punnett
Fresno, California

CONTENTS

PREFACE

This book addresses loneliness and the feeling of being alone in the world, two distinct characteristics that mark the life of an orphan. Regardless if we have grown up with or without parents, we are all too likely to meet such experiences in ourselves and our daily encounters with others. Our technological age has enabled us to create networks with many people, but these relationships often fail to meet the need to belong to someone, some place or something in a world that suffers from "spiritual depletion, emotional alienation, and personal isolation." With numerous case examples, Dr. Punnett describes how loneliness and the feeling of being alone tend to be repeated in later relationships, especially when the earlier attachment patterns have been insecure, disruptive, or intrusive and can eventually lead to pathological states of anxiety and depression.

In an historical survey, Dr. Punnett outlines some of the appalling conditions that parentless children have suffered. One just has to think of 19th century England, as described in the novels of Dickens or the Dying rooms of Asia. Despite Biblical exhortation to care for the homeless and the gradual increased social empathy for orphans, as witnessed in the creation of orphanages and their gradual replacement through foster families, improved outer circumstances fail to bring the kind of healing that makes such devastating experiences meaningful.

A main purpose of this book is not just to stay within the context of the literal orphan, but also to explore its symbolic dimensions, for the author believes that symbols provide meaning to the diverse experiences of feeling alone in the world. Regardless if a child is brought up by parents or not, the orphan complex can be constellated, especially if attachment patterns have been problematic. In order not to remain limited by a purely biographical approach to the psychological orphan, Dr. Punnett elaborates on the archetypal foundations of this complex.

She notes that many heroes have suffered abandonment in childhood. Their birth and early development, usually emerging from miraculous circumstances, bear the characteristics of a Divine Child, symbolizing hope and renewal for the individual, for society, and for our culture.

The constellation of this archetype in dreams, fantasy, and sandplay can act as an inspiration and bring transformation to those who have endured the sufferings of an orphan. With the help of amplification and case material, the author shows in a convincing way how the constellation of the orphan archetype with its accompanying feelings of isolation, anguish, and despair can act as a catalyst for the individuation process. Inspired by Jung's creation of the Orphan Stone in Bollingen, Dr. Punnett's book has placed the orphan at the center rather than at the periphery of human concern and invites us to explore the creative potential in feeling alone in oneself and the world. This is a remarkable book on a subject that tends to be viewed with attitudes that are too narrow and restrictive. The author concludes that in accepting the orphan within, we begin to take responsibility for our own unique life journey, an attitude that also celebrates authentic relationship with the other.

John Hill
Zurich, Switzerland

LIST OF FIGURES

Chapter 1

INTRODUCTION

Orphanus Sum means I am an orphan, alone
C.G. Jung[1]

It was a typical cool spring Halifax evening, a light misty rain was coming down and many people on the streets were walking about sans umbrellas, as if nothing in the slightest was amiss. Coming from warm, sunny California I had on multiple layers as well as raincoat and umbrella in hand, I must have looked a bit different. This was my first time to this part of the country and I was very impressed with this picturesque Atlantic harbor town and the houses nestled about and although I come from the Pacific side of North America, I somehow felt a connection to this land. I was going to give a lecture and seminar the following day on the orphan and I wondered who would come and be interested in such a topic. I had written on this topic that is about the journey we each face of finding significance, meaning and wholeness in our individual lives. And now here I was in a foreign land wondering if this experience would have meaning for others.

According to the organizers of this series, more people than ever had registered for one of these lectures indicating, perhaps, a strong interest in the topic or that perhaps unconsciously many more people than

---

1 C.G. Jung, *Memories, Dreams, Reflections*, p. 216. *MDR* refers throughout this publication to *Memories, Dreams, Reflections*.

I thought were on the journey to finding their own meaning. I was pleased for the organizers and still curious about the participants. At the conclusion of the first talk there were time for questions and a young woman in her 20's shared that she worked in the local shopping mall and was very concerned by the number of people she saw who seemed to be so unhappy and she wondered if there was anything she could do to help these people. She had such compassion for their suffering and I was struck by the maturity of her question. My thought was that she had known suffering of some sort and now had this sensitivity to others. The following day this woman brought a book as a gift to me, *The Thirty-Seven Practices of Bodhisattvas*, and one verse that related to her question and perhaps her sensitivity is as follows:

> Though you lack what you need and are constantly disparaged,
> Afflicted by dangerous sickness and spirits,
> Without discouragement take on the misdeeds
> And the pain of all living beings—
> This is the practice of Bodhisattvas.[2]

This passage reflects that despite the difficulties of living, one must guard against losing mental balance and clarity and not be tempted to turn to drugs or alcohol or return to unhealthy relationships. The suffering we encounter or the sufferings of others that contribute to our troubles can be seen as spiritual teachers helping us to develop greater patience, compassion, love, tolerance, perseverance and free us from the suffering. It was what I had learned about in Switzerland during my analytic training that one must stay with the suffering because it will become our teacher. To ask, "What is the meaning of this for me?" will take us to new consciousness and it is a journey that by its very nature, we must do alone.

In Jungian psychology, "higher consciousness, or knowledge going beyond our present-day consciousness, is equivalent to being *all alone*

---

2 G.S. Rinchen, *The Thirty-Seven Practices of Bodhisattvas*, p. 50.

in the world."[3] It is this sense that 'I am alone' whether I have family or friends around me, and that we are on a journey that takes us to greater meaning that will be the topic of this book. The feeling is one of being alone in the world. *Orphanus Sum* is Latin for 'I am an orphan' and this basic sense of being alone will be explored. Specifically, what do we know about it, where does it come from, how does it become manifest, and what are we to do with the experience of feeling all alone. This feeling is more and more common in our world today, perhaps as a counterbalance to the ease with which one can become "connected" via the Internet and where "relationships" are easily formed.

C.G. Jung explored the orphan when in 1950, in remembrance of his 75th birthday he completed the last face of the cube stone carving at his country home in Bollingen. This stone has particular significance to our topic because it has a quote about the orphan on one side. Jung stated[4] that the saying about the orphan, which he carved, was more or less quotations from alchemy. The exact source has been difficult to uncover, but Dr. Med. Alfred Ribi[5] has researched alchemical texts and found that the text on the stone in Bollingen is "not verbatim quotations from Alchemy." "The orphan first appears in *Pretiosa Margarita Novella* of Petrus Bonus: 'This orphan stone has no proper name.'"[6] The orphan is also in an edition by Janus Lacinius, "...*non est mirandum quoniam hic lapis orphanus proprio nomine caret....*"[7] Translated by Dr. Ribi this says, "No wonder that this stone is called an orphan because it has no name of its own." Thus, the orphan is alone without an identity. Jung stated regarding the passage on the stone he carved that this was the stone speaking, *ego emi*, being personified of himself; it reads translated from the Latin as follows:

---

3   C.G. Jung, The Psychology of the Child Archetype, *The Archetypes of the Collective Unconscious, CW 9i,* ¶ 288. Note: *CW* refers throughout this publication to *The Collected Works of C.G. Jung.*
4   Jung, *MDR.*
5   A. Ribi, personal communication, February 27, 2001.
6   C.G. Jung, The Components of the Coniunctio, *Mysterium Coniunctionis, CW 14,* ¶ 13fn.
7   J. Lacinius, *Pretiosa Margarita Novella de Thesauro ac Pretiosissimo Philosophorum Lapide,* p. 54r.

I am an orphan, alone; nevertheless I am found everywhere. I am one, but opposed to myself. I am youth and old man at one and the same time. I have known neither father nor mother, because I have had to be fetched out of the deep like a fish, or fell like a white stone from heaven. In woods and mountains I roam, but I am hidden in the innermost soul of man. I am mortal for everyone, yet I am not touched by the cycle of aeons.[8]

Maude Oakes, a painter-writer, amateur anthropologist and cousin of the man who was making a film about Jung, wanted to understand the meaning of the carving and set to the task of discovering its significance. She met with Jung at Bollingen a few years after he had finished carving the stone. She had been asked to analyze the significance of the stone for the film, and it was in this context she began her research.

In the initial conversation with Jung about the stone he remarked, "The Stone is nothing. I am not an artist; I did it to amuse myself. It is a holiday thing—as if I sang a song."[9] Miss Oakes then corresponded with Jung regarding her manuscript on the book about the stone and he replied that all the volumes he had written were contained in the stone. He talked about the symbols on the stone and remarked, "They are mere allusions, they hint at something, they stammer and often lose their way. They are nothing but humble attempts to formulate, to define, to shape the inexpressible." They were not to be read as "sort of a confession of a belief,"[10] and Jung denied ever being any proprietor of metaphysical truths. Jung also went on to say how important the feeling and local atmosphere were to the stone and that it belonged to its secluded place between the lake and the hill, where it expressed the *beata solitudo*[11] and the *genus loci*.[12] "Only there in its solitude it can say: *Orphanus sum* and only there it [the stone] makes sense."[13] This has implications for one's

---

8   Jung, *MDR*, p. 216.
9   M. Oakes, *The Stone Speaks: The Memoir of a Personal Transformation*, p. 15.
10 Oakes, *The Stone Speaks*, p. 18.
11 D.P. Simpson, *Cassell's Latin Dictionary*, p. 74.
12 Simpson, *Cassell's Latin Dictionary*, pp. 264, 349.
13 Oakes, *The Stone Speaks*, p. 19.

own journey because our histories are influenced by the parents we had and the locale of our upbringing.

The orphan carving faces the lake at Bollingen and has been captured by a photo published in Jaffe's book (Figure 1).[14]

Figure 1. The stone at Bollingen.
Source: Jaffe, 1979, p. 204.

Recently, the stone has been given a hood to protect it from the elements and is pictured in its solitude amidst the mountains and the lake (Figure 2).

---

14   A. Jaffe, *Word and Image*, p. 204.

Figure 2. The stone with copper cover.
Photo by A. F. Punnett.

Jung stated, the stone "…is there for its own sake and only seen by a few. Under such conditions only, the stone will whisper its misty lore of ancient roots and ancestral lives."[15] Although she was trying to understand what Jung meant by his carvings on the stone, he told her she could only discover its meaning by looking at what the stone meant to her. She took this seriously and in the process discovered the parable of her own inner life, her own search and discovery, which is the most significant aspect of the text from the alchemists. That is, that one's own journey, despite whatever suffering it entails, is an individual journey and must be honored for the product of the inner change that occurs over a lifetime. Jung thought this was achieved not by analysis, but by synthesis leading to integration; one's life has a teleological significance and that which we encounter leads us to achieving wholeness. And when we experience the suffering we are alone, like the orphan, yet this is what the orphan is called to do.

15 Oakes, *The Stone Speaks*, p. 19.

Jung began on a journey of self-exploration through his years of work, which is now published in *The Red Book: Liber Novus*. He wrote,

> The years, of which I have spoken to you, when I pursued the inner images, were the most important time of my life. Everything else is to be derived from this. It began at that time, and the later details hardly matter anymore. My entire life consisted in elaborating what had burst forth from the unconscious and flooded me like an enigmatic stream and threatened to break me. That was the stuff and material for more than only one life. Everything later was merely the outer classification, the scientific elaboration, and the integration into life. But the numinous beginning, which contained everything, was then.[16]

In a section called "the Desert," Jung describes the importance of being with oneself. Not just the self that is caught up with daily ideas, but the place where "torment" belongs, a place where one turns to the "spirit of the depths that turns to the things of the soul, the world of the soul."[17] Jung goes on to say, " Only the self enters in there, or the man who has completely become his self, he who is neither events, nor in men, nor in his thoughts." In this place Jung further reasoned that one had to detach oneself from thoughts and to give patience to the fertile soil that would emerge which when "…the creative force now turns to the place of the soul, you will see how your soul becomes green and how its field bears wonderful fruit." Jung likened this waiting for the creative forces, as "torment" and that most would be unable to bear this. In order to embark on such a journey, trust must be there: that there is truth in the images that come when one enters the solitude of the desert as the ancients have done before us.

Therefore, one has potential, the capacity to become or develop into something in the future. The word potential comes from the late Middle English and from the late Latin *potentialis* meaning to have power.[18]

---

16 Jung, *The Red Book: Liber Novus*, vii.
17 Jung, *The Red Book*, p. 236.
18 E. Klein, *A Comprehensive Etymological Dictionary of the English Language, Unabridged, One-Volume Edition*, p. 580.

These are potentials that exist in all of us, but it is a hero's journey to acquire such learning from this being with oneself, to understand what one is about and the place one has to be in the world.

There are many facets to the orphan, from the images that are evoked of the parentless child who carried society's shadow and shame[19] to the process by which an individual becomes more differentiated and conscious to not only his outer but inner world. This feeling of being different, not understood, and/or not fitting in with family or friends provokes the feeling of being alone in the world. Recently, there has been much research looking at neurobiology and the importance of the mother-child dyad, and while this has implications for the feeling of being alone, it is not the entire answer. It is larger than biological factors and needs to encompass the culture and the innate heritage of human-kind. The journey is about the human ability to untie humankind from whatever the early circumstances were to acquire consciousness, and this transcends location and culture because it belongs to the collective unconscious and exists as an archetype. With that in mind, we will look at what the concept of orphan could mean symbolically. The fairy tale, "The Little Orphan Girl" will be discussed and interpreted to illustrate what this might look like in a person today. Personal stories throughout will demonstrate the complexities of that feeling of being alone in the world.

The orphan stands alone and has on the one hand a potential for growth and new beginnings, and on the other hand, the potential for remaining isolated and on the outside. The tension of these opposite poles, potential to isolation, perhaps gives the orphan within us an even greater opportunity for reconciliation. The child or adult who is alone has the potential for an extraordinary adventure, which is the archetypal truth of the orphan. Let us begin by looking at the historical context of the orphan.

---

19   J. Evetts-Secker, *Orphanos Exoikos: The Precarious Possibility of Wholeness.*

Chapter 2

THE HISTORICAL CONTEXT OF THE ORPHAN

Although, I am not disposed to maintain that the being born in a workhouse, is in itself the most fortunate and enviable circumstance that can possibly befall a human being, I do mean to say in this particular instance, it was the best thing for Oliver Twist that could by possibility have occurred.

Charles Dickens[20]

As a backdrop to this chapter, it may be of interest to know how I came to write about the orphan. Basically, the orphan found me! I had gone to Switzerland, alone, to study at the C.G. Jung Institute in Küsnacht.

While in Switzerland, I made friends in the international community and it was through these connections opportunities arose. Some of my friends' children were involved in a play about Janusz Korczak's life, and I attended the performance. Korczak, a Jew, was born in Warsaw and became a pediatrician who also wrote books that gained him some literary recognition. Later he became a mentor for orphaned children as director of *Dorn Sierot*, the orphanage of his own design for Jewish children.[21] When the Germans created the Warsaw Ghetto in 1940, he was forced to move the orphanage there. At one point, the German soldiers came to collect the orphans and Korczak refused to leave them despite opportunities to remain behind; instead he went with them to their

---

20   C. Dickens, *Oliver Twist*, p. 1.
21   http://en.wikipedia.org/wiki/Janusz_Korczak

death at the Treblinka extermination camp. The play was very moving and spoke to the dedication Korczak felt toward these children who had no parents, and to his authenticity as a person. This also spoke to me about his solitary journey to follow a calling, which was so against the wishes of his peers, and the collective.

My interest in the orphan was peaked from this play primarily because I was on such a solitary journey and felt like an orphan in a foreign land, not really belonging; yet I was there. However, I knew that this was the journey I had to be on and being alone made it all the more poignant to discover more about myself. Talking about my interest in the orphan with friends and acquaintances led to an interview with a man who was introduced to me because he had been in an orphanage in Switzerland. I was so curious to find out about his journey and his survival. He was open and honest and had survived a significant disruption in his life due to World War II. Yet, it was not the end of him and albeit alone, he was stronger for the experience and had made a good life for himself and his family in Switzerland.

Shortly after this I had an opportunity to visit Oxford to attend a Jungian lecture for The Guild of Pastoral Psychology. After the lecture, there were used books for sale scattered on a large round wooden table. Always interested in any book, I began to survey them and to my surprise there was a book titled, *The Stone Speaks: The Memoir of a Personal Transformation*.[22] It gave me goose bumps as I opened the book and saw a photograph of Jung's carving of the orphan stone. The synchronicity of finding this book became more and more profound. Then I knew I must visit Bollingen, the home of the stone.

Coincidentally, the Jung family opened up Bollingen once per year to students enrolled in the Institute! There I found the stone, which did not belong and on which Jung carved the orphan quote detailed in the first chapter. It seemed now with all these opportunities having arisen within a short period of time that this was what I must write about, and it so resonated with my own journey. This was a personal meandering, and what seemed like an aimless wandering began to have meaning.

---

22 Oakes, *The Stone Speaks*.

This is an example of what Jung talks about when one is on their path, doors will open to us that we had not imagined.

Definition

In Hebrew orphan, יתום, *yāthôm,* is defined as אין אב, *ain āb,* 'fatherless' and quotes from the Bible suggested these people were helpless, exposed to injury. For example in Exodus 22:24, "… and your wives shall become widows, and your children fatherless." Nevertheless, from this use of the Hebrew word in the Bible, it is not clear that both parents were dead.[23] Hebrew law carefully provided for the fatherless children with special tithes at the end of every three-year period and the requirement that gleanings be left in the fields for them. Deuteronomy, 14:28, "At the end of every three years you shall bring forth all the tithe of your produce in the same year, and lay it up within your towns; and…the fatherless, and the widow…shall come eat and be filled." The plea to care for the fatherless child is frequent and often associated with the widow in order that compassion be shown for the needy. Exodus 22:22, "You shall not afflict any widow or orphan" and Deuteronomy 10:17-18, "For the Lord your God is god of gods and Lord of lords, the great, the mighty, and the terrible God, who…executes justice for the fatherless and the widow…."

The word orphan is derived from the Latin, *orphanus,* and from the Greek, ὀρφανός, which translates as the adjective, "fatherless," "orphaned."[24] The original meaning was not that both parents were absent, but only that the father was missing. Although there is not clear documentation, the fatherless could have been a daughter, and in those times she only inherited from her father in the absence of sons. Thus, the fatherless daughters required special consideration in the Israelite community. It has been suggested that the fatherless were female children of sacred prostitutes, who had no identified father. Their life was integrated with the temple and sometimes barren women adopted these

---

23 Brown, Driver & Briggs, *Hebrew and English Lexicon of the Old Testament,* p. 450.
24 J. Hastings, *A Dictionary of the Bible, Vol. 3,* p. 634.

children.[25] Currently, *The Concise Oxford Dictionary* defines orphan as a child bereaved of a parent or usually both parents.[26]

Interestingly, the word "individual" is etymologically related to the word "widow."[27] According to Klein,[28] widow (Latin *vidua*) derives from *di-videre* meaning to "divide" and from the Indo-European base *widh-* "to separate." Thus, widow means the parted one and therefore prior to widowhood one is still subject to the parting process, not yet an individual. Even though women have been the focus, this also extends to the widower, because men also have the experience of being widowed and of this feeling of being alone in the world. The point is that a person must be parted from that on which he or she is dependent in order to be an individual. As we will see later, becoming an individual means becoming differentiated and less and less dependent on another human being. And, of course, the importance of this is being true to one's own nature and one's own unique destiny.

This is not an easy task and an illustration of this is evident in a man who lost his wife after 22 years of marriage. Bob's story is common, although his suffering was pronounced as he moved through the grief of her death. At 58 years of age, Bob had waited to find the right person to marry, and while the marriage was considered a good one, there were communication difficulties that were not addressed and complacency developed. These were the kind of encounters that one often dismisses in service of the relationship, but over time these missed opportunities for communication begin to diminish the relationship. In the family, an overly close relationship with the eldest son and mother developed such that the son became more dependent on her for his emotional needs, telephoning everyday while he was away at college. Bob tried to make comments, but they went unheeded and then when she died the son went into a significant depression. Bob now had to look at his part in this and how he dismissed his needs and colluded with this arrangement, how the marriage was not "perfect," and how he had to face his

25 *Interpreter's Dictionary of the Bible, Vol. 2*, pp. 245-6.
26 R.E. Allen, *The Concise Oxford Dictionary of Current English*, p. 838.
27 E.F. Edinger, *Ego and Archetype*.
28 *A Comprehensive Etymological Dictionary of the English Language, Unabridged, One-Volume Edition*, p. 827.

loneliness to build a new life for himself. Bob had to face his fear of being alone, of becoming an individual whose identity did not depend on or was defined by the relationship to another human being.

According to Jung,[29] "Loneliness does not come from having no people about one, but from being unable to communicate the things that seem important to oneself, or from holding certain views which others find inadmissible." This is what happened to Bob and his wife and now what had been unsaid becomes even more profound when the other is gone. There were no more chances for continued conversations to work through the feelings and yet there was opportunity for growth, to understand what went awry and what his part was in the missed communications or how he did not make clear his feelings. It was through the therapy that he could assess the unspoken, realize his passivity in the relationship, and to be heard and validated and no longer feel the acute loneliness that plagued him.

This was also true for William who was married over 30 years when his wife died. While she was diagnosed with cancer and despite treatment and failure to respond, neither of them talked of her impending death. Hospital staff and professionals made attempts to encourage them to communicate, but he rejected these becoming angry at the idea his wife would lose this battle, and she also did not speak up. Now since her death he clings to her memory, and all the unspoken talks they could have had, and he looks for the woman who will fill her place. He remains tied to her memory and negates his own individuality and the potential that exists within him to lead the individual life. This is a crucial time, because it can be so easy to want to replace the departed one without experiencing the renewed strength that can come from this kind of loss and from facing life alone. Ideally the couple will be able to support the other's individual life, not cling or be dependent, making it all the more important to know oneself.

After several years and even though he was dating, William still clung to the memory of his wife finding it difficult to commit to another woman. He looked to replace the closeness he had with his wife, but

---

29 Jung, *MDR*, pp. 327-328.

no woman ever measured up. He had the following dream while with a lover one night:

> I was asleep and I saw a vision of my wife. She was in a bed alone with a blanket pulled up to mid-chest, with her arms under the covers. I looked closely, but I could not tell if she was sleeping or if she was dead, but she did seem to be slightly breathing. I was not sure.
>
> I look to my left and I see my wife sitting down, with maybe her head resting on her fist sort of like the Rodin statue of the Thinker. I see that she acknowledges me. I look at her and say: "I want to be with you."
>
> My wife has gotten up, come over to me and has put her arm around me. She holds her arm around my shoulder and says gently: "I cannot be with you," or maybe "You may not be with me." In a flash I am defensive, and a bit defiant. She looks at me ... and I say to myself, "Oh yes I can. I can be with you...if I want to...I can commit suicide."

From this dream he reported waking up scared and sobbing. He denied any suicidal thoughts, and in fact felt like he was starting to have some fun in his life, but the dream was so real and his wife seemed so life-like that he knew this was an important dream.

While he says he is moving on, it is clear he had not emotionally let go of his wife. And yet she (his anima) is trying to help him "gently" realize he needs to let her go. His stubbornness is relentless to the point of sacrificing his own life. And if he does not come to some new awareness, he will sacrifice the opportunity to live his life with full consciousness. This dream is really a wake-up call for him to understand the dynamics of their relationship and the opportunity to move into new relationships that have potential for intimacy, perhaps in a way he has not known before. He knows he is not ready to make a commitment to another woman and he must ultimately give up trying to replace what he had with this wife. He needs to understand why he so desperately clings to her and yet it is clear that he needs to let go and move on into his own life and to live his destiny.

This is all too common a story with couples that have lived a lifetime together. A woman whose husband died after 50 years of marriage, began to have symptoms of vertigo, a sensation of whirling and loss of balance, nine days after her husband's death. These symptoms remained after numerous medical interventions without relief and then psychotherapy was recommended. The nine represents a new beginning and holds the potential for a more differentiated conscious level, one that will be at one with itself and the world.[30] But is she up for the work this entails? Her husband's death has rendered her incapacitated to do things independently and now rather than being dependent on her husband she has become dependent upon her grown children. Her grief is significant and she sees no purpose to her individual life. She has a very understanding family, that caters to her and does not see the potential for her healing, and her dependency needs are great making the prognosis for change guarded at best. So to understand the grief and suffering, she must go to the desert to experience the depths of her soul and the meaning of her life and now she has an opportunity. This is no easy task!

These feelings of being alone can happen at any age. Danny was a 5-year-old boy who was referred because he was exhibiting "nervous habits' that had not gone away despite behavioral interventions by his parents. The tics consisted of twisting his ears and yawning. The onset of these symptoms came approximately six months after the birth of his sister. The parents at that time were becoming concerned regarding the sister's hearing and she was subsequently diagnosed with a profound congenital hearing loss. The sister's needs became the focus and there were multiple doctor visits and later a surgery. Danny had just begun attending a new school for Kindergarten and was becoming increasingly argumentative. Danny told me a "really scary dream" in which people with flashlights were looking for Thomas, the train[31] in a dark tunnel, "like a ghost tunnel." This dream highlighted his feelings of being alone and needing to be found; the latest tic was symbolically related to the sister's diagnosis.

Over the course of six months, Danny's symptoms resolved once his feelings of abandonment and loss of the mother's attention to his sister

30   T. Abt, *Introduction to Picture Interpretation: According to C.G. Jung.*
31   W. Awdry, *Thomas, the Tank Engine.*

were addressed. He played in the sand and enacted a hero's journey to recapture his personal strength, voice his anger at the mother symbolically and then he could move back into his life. He was affected by the interruption of the relationship with his mother and the understandable medical needs of his sister. According to De Vries,[32] the ear is inquisitiveness and the seat of memory is in the lobe. He resorted to a psychological defense of over-control of his emotions, which was a style modeled for him at home.[33] The parental style was addressed and the parents became more open to listening to feelings and acknowledging them with the presenting symptoms remitting.

Well-known Orphans

Generally, when we think of orphans, we are reminded of their stories in literature. Frequently, they are exposed on the streets with harlots and robbers and covered with soot. They struggle to survive and have the vitality and resourcefulness to either do without or to create their own supply. None is more poignant than the birth of Oliver Twist to an unwed mother who dies after giving birth to him. From the start he is initiated into being alone in the world. There is also the unwanted child who has to struggle with the value of his own existence. Mark Twain's Huckleberry Finn refuses pity and care and prefers to be on his own. J. K. Rowling's Harry Potter becomes an orphan after losing both parents and struggles with finding a place where he can fit in given his unique talents.

The Harry Potter books, first published in 1997, captivated contemporary culture for many years. Why? First of all, there were seven books and the number seven seems to be connected to man's unconscious soul and his spiritual development, which as it turns out is a major theme of the books. Harry is an orphan and the series chronicles Harry's battles against the satanic figure, Voldemort, a French word meaning flight of death. Harry survived the attack of his parents and Voldemort's attempt to kill him. He is left with a lightning-bolt scar on his forehead, a symbol of Zeus' capacity for creation and destruction. This is the first evi-

---

32 *Dictionary of Symbols and Imagery.*
33 A.F. Punnett, *Journal of Sandplay Therapy,* 18, 1, pp. 27-45.

dence of his shamanic calling, and that as an orphan he is called to greater things. Marie-Louise von Franz states we must take the hero-child within its archetypal context, because then it takes on a much deeper meaning, "namely that the new God of our time is always to be found in the ignored and deeply unconscious corner of the psyche." She goes on to say, "If an individual has got to suffer a neurosis as a result of being an abandoned child, he or she is called upon to turn toward the abandoned God within but not to identify with his suffering."[34]

We learn there was a prophecy that Harry's and Voldemort's lives were bound together, the good and the evil, and that neither can live while the other survives. This is first noted in the link between the magic wands they both use, which have a pair of feathers from a phoenix tail, and it was this wand that scared Harry. Thus, it becomes a spiritual journey, when Harry realizes he must sacrifice himself willingly in order to save the world from Voldemort and in so doing he dies, comes back and remains nonviolent to the end of Voldemort's death by his own rebounding death curse. Harry's journey was an individual one, and he models for us that all of our actions have eternal consequences. This is in stark contrast to the consumerism so prevalent today in which one's needs can be met by material possessions. In this technological world there is spiritual depletion, emotional alienation and personal isolation and it is only through trying to understand our place in this complex world that we can begin to make some sense. In effect our choices define who we are and our destiny to live that, hopefully, strives for the greater good.

Even previous to these contemporary stories, we have stories from the Bible, which are significant for the struggle to exist and to live out a fated destiny. One such story is that of Moses. Another story from Roman mythology is that of Romulus.

Moses

As a way of background, in the first chapter of Exodus, Pharaoh commanded his people to throw into the Nile all sons that were born to

---

34 M-L. von Franz, *Interpretation of Fairy Tales*, p. viii.

the Hebrews (the daughters were permitted to live). The reason for this order seemed to be concern of over-fertility of the Israelites whom they feared, but also a prophecy that a son born to the Israelites would destroy all Egypt.

The events preceding Moses' birth give even further light to what was to come. The following story comes from Hebrew mythology.[35] In the sixtieth year after Joseph's death, the reigning Pharaoh had a dream in which he saw an old man who held a pair of scales. All the inhabitants of Egypt lie on one side and a suckling lamb, which outweighed all the Egyptians, lie on the other. The dream was declared to mean that a son would be born to the Israelites who would destroy all Egypt. The Pharaoh was frightened and at once ordered the death of all newborn male children of the Israelites in the entire country. Due to this order, the Levite, Amram, decided to separate from his wife, Jochebed, so that certain death would not befall the children conceived by him. His daughter, Miriam, who told with prophetic assurance that the child in the Pharaoh's dream would come from her mother's womb and would become the liberator of his people, opposed this resolution. With this Amram rejoined his wife, from whom he had been separated for three years. At the end of three months, she conceived the son who was later to be called Moses. At his birth, it was told that the entire house was illuminated by an extraordinary radiance, suggesting the truth of the prophecy.

The biblical birth story of Moses is told in the second chapter of Exodus.

> Now a man from the house of Levi went and took to wife a daughter of Levi. The woman conceived and bore a son; and when she saw that he was a goodly child, she hid him three months. And when she could hide him no longer she took for him a basket made of bulrushes, and daubed it with bitumen and pitch; and she put the child in it and placed it among the reeds at the river's brink. And his sister stood at a distance, to know what would be done to him. Now the daughter of Pharaoh came down to bathe at the river, and her

---

35   O. Rank, *In Quest of the Hero.*

maidens walked beside the river; she saw the basket among the reeds and sent her maid to fetch it. When she opened it she saw the child; and lo, the babe was crying. She took pity on him and said, 'This is one of the Hebrews' children.' Then his sister said to Pharaoh's daughter, 'Shall I go and call you a nurse from the Hebrew women to nurse the child for you?' And Pharaoh's daughter said to her, 'Go.' So the girl went and called the child's mother. And Pharaoh's daughter said to her, 'Take this child away, and nurse him for me, and I will give you your wages.' So the woman took the child and nursed him. And the child grew, and she brought him to Pharaoh's daughter, and he became her son; and she named him Moses, for she said, 'Because I drew him out of the water.' (Exodus 2:1-10, Revised Standard Version)

Interestingly, in the story, while he is separated from his mother, it is she who comes to nurse him until he is then given to the Pharaoh's daughter. In those days nursing was most likely carried on for at least two years.[36] Regardless, Moses was considered an orphan because he was ultimately without his biological mother and father. This orphanhood comes to underscore the journey that he must take, that is, a very individual and intentional journey to increased consciousness. Romanelli captures Moses being found in the bullrushes in a painting (Figure 3).

Thus, Moses, is a legend because he was "…the mediating agent between Yahweh and Israel [who] brings about the redemption of his people from Egyptian bondage and leads the nation to fulfillment of its destiny."[37] Moses had the characteristics of the myth of the birth of the hero as exemplified by: "1) the birth occurs under adverse circumstances; 2) the authorities seek to kill it; 3) the infant is exposed or abandoned, often in water; 4) the person is rescued, usually by lowly people, and accompanied by marvels; 5) there is a double set of parents, royal ones and lowly ones."[38] In relating this as a metaphor to the individual psyche, the

---

36 Klaus & Kennell, *Parent-Infant Bonding.*

37 E.F. Edinger, *The Bible and the Psyche: Individuation Symbolism in the Old Testament*, p. 45.

38 Edinger, *The Bible and the Psyche*, pp. 45-46.

person through an intuitive process discovers his or her innate wisdom and pattern of being, and this will entail learning that one has limita-

Figure 3. Moses rescued from the water
by Giovanni Francesco Romanelli. Source: Bridgeman Art Library.
Reprinted by permission.

tions. These limitations, and ultimately the need for death,[39] give meaning and where mastery in this life is to be found, and therefore, restriction is freedom. Thus, one becomes an orphan in order that his or her life might be saved and have meaning.

Romulus

This is a Roman myth of the hero Romulus. The child is a twin and in this story is of royal lineage but the current ruler condemns him and his brother to be thrown into the river only later to be suckled by a female animal and once discovered, they are raised by a couple whose only child had died. The myth's main theme is one of overcoming initial adversity.

The birth of the twins came about after King Proca gave his kingdom to his first-born son, Numitor. However, his younger brother, Amulius, pushed him from the throne and became king himself. So that none of Numitor's progeny could claim the throne, Amulius killed all his male descendents. Numitor's daughter, Ilia, was made a vestal virgin, but she succumbed to a relationship (unknown who he was), named Mars as the father of her illegitimate offspring.

> The twins borne by Ilia, the daughter of the preceding king Numitor, from the embrace of the war-god Mars were condemned by King Amulius, the present ruler of Alba, to be cast into the river. The king's servants took the children and carried them from Alba as far as the Tiber on the Palatine Hill; but when they tried to descend the hill to the river, to carry out the command, they found that the river had risen, and they were unable to reach its bed. The tub with the children was therefore thrust by them into the shallow water at the shore. It floated for a while; but the water promptly receded, and knocking against a stone, the tub capsized, and the screaming infants were upset into the river mud. They were heard by a she-wolf who had just brought forth and had her udders full of milk; she came and gave her teats to the boys, to nurse them, and as they were drinking she licked them clean with her tongue. Above them flew a woodpecker, which guarded the children, and also carried food to them.

---

39 Jung, *The Red Book.*

Figure 4. Romulus and Remus by Charles de Lafosse. Source:
Bridgeman Art Library. Reprinted by permission.

The father was providing for her sons: for the wolf and the
woodpecker are animals consecrated to father Mars. This was
seen by one of the royal herdsmen, who was driving his pigs
back to the pasture from which the water had receded. Star-
tled by the spectacle, he summoned his mates, who found
the she-wolf attending like a mother to the children, and the
children treated her as their mother. [See painting by Lafosse,
Figure 4.]

The men made a loud noise to scare the animal away; but the
wolf was not afraid; she left the children, but not from fear;
slowly, without heeding the herdsmen, she disappeared into
the wilderness of the forest, at the holy site of Faunus, where
the water gushes from a gully of the mountain. [The famous
Etruscan bronze, fifth century BC captures the she-wolf feed-
ing the twins, Figure 5.]

Figure 5. The Capitoline She-Wolf with figures of Romulus and
Remus by Antonio Pollaiuolo. Source: Bridgeman Art Library.
Reprinted by permission.

Meanwhile the men picked up the boys and carried them to
the chief swineherd of the king, Faustulus, for they believed
that the gods did not wish the children to perish. But the
wife of Faustulus had just given birth to a dead child, and
was full of sorrow. Her husband gave her the twins, and she
nursed them; the couple raised the children, and named them
Romulus and Remus.[40]

With respect to the Romulus tale, it is highly probable that the original story told only of Romulus, while the figure of Remus was added
later.[41] This may have been in relation to the twin myths of hostile brothers. Edinger states with respect to twins, "…that the ego destined for
individuation is born as twins." This is in relation to the legend that

---

40 Rank, *Quest of the Hero*, pp. 34-35.
41 Rank, *Quest of the Hero*.

twins embodied good and evil and hence a split and needed reconcilia-tion. "This division into two has two aspects: ego and shadow, and ego and Self."[42]

And why would one be destined for individuation? The characteris-tics of the hero's journey were mentioned, and to go on the hero's jour-ney means that one becomes more conscious of one's shadow; the ego is not in ultimate control, and that one listens to the urgings of the Self which may be in contrast to society's expectations or even our own (ego-driven) expectations. Here in the twin motif one can see psychologically the work that needs to be done.

Regardless, the twins were rescued from the river and brought to Faustulus where they were raised by he and his wife. When they were grown to manhood, Remus was one day accused of having stolen Numi-tor's flock. Numitor was now the king since his brother Amulius had been assassinated and to whom Remus was taken. Numitor suspects this is his grandchild. Soon Romulus arrives and a conspiracy is created to which the boys seek vengeance and their rightful throne. However, since neither knows who was first born, Remus tries to deride his brother who becomes so enraged that he kills him. Romulus becomes king and the city Rome was named after him.

These two legends were about orphans who had precarious begin-nings, yet vitality and resourcefulness became apparent. Each man came from a different social class, yet both were called to go beyond these dif-ficult beginnings. This is not only a fate, when it remains unconscious, but also a destiny, when it becomes conscious, and it can relate to not only the time in which we are brought up, but also the parents we are given. Both of these possibilities will be discussed.

The Orphan in History

To understand the plight of the orphan, it is helpful to understand the cultural attitudes of raising children, which has evolved over the centu-ries. This gives a context for understanding how children and ultimately the orphan were given attention over the centuries and the impact of

---

42 Edinger, *Bible and the Psyche*, p. 36.

culture upon the development of the individual, which has received notice with the publication of Joseph Henderson's book, *Cultural Attitudes in Psychological Perspective*,[43] and more attention recently with the publication of *The Cultural Complex: Contemporary Jungian Perspectives on Psyche and Society*.[44] There has been an evolving cultural attitude, which seems to have influenced a psychological attitude towards more empathy and more feeling for the child. De Mause[45] divided parent-child relationships in the course of European history into a series of six categories. These categories show progression toward the capacity for empathic parental responsiveness to the child. At the very least this sets the context for how children and ultimately the orphan were given attention over the centuries.

1. Infanticide (Antiquity to Fourth Century A.D.): Parents routinely resolved their anxieties about taking care of children by killing them. The child receives the projection that whatever happens is his/her fault.

2. Abandonment (Fourth to Thirteenth Century A.D.): Parents begin to accept that children have a soul. However, the child continues to receive projections of evil. Parents escape their anxieties by giving the child away or emotionally abandoning it at home.

3. Ambivalence (Fourteenth to Seventeenth Century): Parents believe it is their task to mold and shape the child, both mentally and physically. Parents attempt to be more personal, but this only serves to intensify parental ambivalence between love and rejection. There is an increase in the number of child instruction books.

4. Intrusion (Eighteenth Century): The child was no longer so full of dangerous projections during this time. Parents approached the child in attempts to control its will, anger, needs, and even its bodily functions. Empathy begins to develop, as the child is not seen as such a threat.

5. Socialization (Nineteenth to mid-Twentieth Century): As projections continued to decrease, raising a child became less a process of conquering its will to training, guiding and socializing. Now child-

---

43 J.L. Henderson, *Cultural Attitudes in Psychological Perspective*.

44 Singer & Kimbles, *The Cultural Complex: Contemporary Jungian Perspectives on Psyche and Society*.

45 L. De Mause, *The History of Childhood*.

hood as a concept begins to exist with the potential for idealization. The father for the first time begins to take more than a casual interest in the child.

6. Support (from the mid-Twentieth Century): This form of child rearing is based on the premise that the child knows better than the parent what it needs in each stage of its life. Both parents are involved in empathizing with and expanding the child's needs.

It was not until the outlawing of infanticide by early Christianity that there was a need for institutions where the abandoned and the orphaned were looked after. There were attempts to protect the orphaned from being sold into slavery in Rome, but this only occurred under benevolent rulers. In the Twelfth Century, at a time when life expectancy was only thirty years, many children lost their parents early. Guy de Montpellier established the Order of the Holy Spirit to look after these children. When Pope Innocent III arrived in Rome, he was appalled by the number of babies' bodies floating in the Tiber that he asked de Montpellier to spread the work of his Order in Italy.[46]

Figure 6. Foundling Hospital of the Innocents, Roundel from the façade by Andrea della Robbia. Source: Bridgeman Art Library. Reprinted by permission.

46 E. Simpson, *Orphans: Real and Imaginary.*

In foundling homes and orphanages like Florence's famous Innocenti, (see the rounded detail from the façade of The Foundling Hospital of the Innocents, Figure 6) peasant women nursed the babies either inside or outside the orphanage. In Paris, a mother deposits her child at the Foundling Hospital, Figure 7.

Figure 7. Mother Depositing Her Child in the Foundling Hospital in Paris by Henry Nelson O'Neil. Source: Bridgeman Art Library. Reprinted by permission.

These children lived in the orphanage until ages seven or eight and then they were either adopted or sent out as apprentices and servants.

Until the Reformation, it was the clergy or lay workers under the supervision of the Order who took care of orphans. In countries where the convents or monasteries were shut down, the orphans again became vagrants. In England with the passage of the Poor Relief Act under Elizabeth I, the state took responsibility for the orphans and placed them under the jurisdiction of community nurseries.[47] Here they were looked after until they were old enough to be placed elsewhere. Emma Brownlow depicts orphans being christened in her painting entitled 'The Christening,' Figure 8.

Figure 8. The Christening by Emma Brownlow. Source:
Bridgeman Art Library. Reprinted by permission.

During the Industrial Revolution, there was an increase in the orphan population, which resulted in changes in their care. This increase was a

47 Simpson, *Orphans*.

result of the migration from farms to cities; unemployment, poverty, and overcrowding resulted in many parentless children on the street, including children turned out by indigent parents. There were so many on the streets that the gentry wanted them put away and so they were thrown into almshouses with the impoverished, insane, and depraved adults.

The orphaned king, Edward VI, recognized the need to institutionalize children separately when he established the Blue Coat School at Christ's Hospital in Newgate, England, in the middle of the Sixteenth Century. Edward's mother died 12 days after his birth and he was considered King Henry VIII's only legitimate son; he ascended the throne when he was a mere nine years old.[48] Perhaps his own developmental history sensitized him to the needs of others. Reportedly, the School went through phases during which the governing of the children was benign or brutal, depending on the interest the reigning monarch took in its management. The patronizing attitude of the public toward these orphans was suggested by the custom of using them to swell funeral processions. By the late Eighteenth Century, some children were sent to these orphanages because their parents were abroad in the colonies or for some other reason could not keep them at home. At this point in time, the "orphans" were taught by superior masters who prepared them for a university education. It was no longer a "common orphan school."

All of this within the context of the changing family, as we know, evolved very slowly from the end of the feudal period to the modern era. Until the Seventeenth and Eighteenth Century, the structure of the family remained loose and its emotional tone, especially in England, remained cool. Infants were routinely under the care of wet nurses. At age seven, dressed and treated like adults, they moved into the adult world. As previously discussed, neglect and ill treatment of the young were commonplace at a time when childhood as a stage of life was not honored. A child without parents was little worse off than the one with parents and so many were orphaned early that their circumstances were not noteworthy.[49]

---

48 *The New Encyclopedia Britannica*, p. 378.
49 Simpson, *Orphans*.

By the middle of the Nineteenth Century and the era of the bourgeois family reached its peak, the middle and upper-class children were pampered as never before and this was when the contrast to the orphan became so apparent. The attention to the orphan became the subject in novels and attracted the attention of social reformers.

Figure 9. Poster advertising the film, 'L 'Enfant de Paris produced
by Gaumont Cinema Films. Source: Bridgeman Art Library.
Reprinted by permission.

In London, Lord Shaftesbury established the Ragged School Union which was named after a model orphanage established in 1695 by August Francke in Halle, Germany. Charles Dickens wrote novels which exposed the evils of almshouses and the corruption of the heads of orphanages as well as the cruelty of couples to whom the children were bound. Films depicted orphans as seen in the poster advertising the 'L 'Enfant de Paris,' Figure 9 and book covers as well as seen in Figure 10.

Figure 10. "Frozen Out" children's book cover by Mabel Lucie Attwell. Source: Bridgeman Art Library & Mabel Lucie Attwell © Lucie Attwell Ltd. Reprinted by permission.

With the opening of the New World, vagrant children were gathered by agents and exported to the Colonies in America to provide inexpensive labor. Almshouses and orphanages were opened by the states and by religious orders especially as the need for them increased as a result of epidemics of yellow fever, cholera, and typhus. As a result of increased immigration after the Civil War in the United States, the number of almshouses and orphanages increased by 300 percent.[50] In 1825 there were two orphan asylums in New York State and by 1866 there were sixty. Even so these institutions were not enough to take care of the homeless children and they again swarmed the city streets.

"Orphan Trains" were organized by the Children's Aid Society[51] to transport the cities' orphans to families out West who were willing to take them in. Upon arrival at their destination, the orphan-train children were greeted by a crowd of applicants who looked them over and made their selections. From 1854 to 1924, an estimated 100,000 children were sent West on these orphan-trains. Many of these foster parents had little or no tolerance for the imperfections of character that biological parents might take for granted. In truth, they were looking more for farmhands and servants than children and little time was allowed for schooling. Some of the foster parents were harsh with them, some orphans ran away, and if the abuse was learned about, the child was transferred to another home. However, the majority of the orphans stayed on until they were able to go out on their own; some were adopted.

News of the abuses of these orphan-train children reached the officials slowly, if at all, but rumors of mismanagement of asylums circulated continually. Investigations were held and resulted in asylum directors printing material showing carefully dressed children seated at well-set tables or playing in the garden. In truth, even minor infractions of the rules resulted in severe punishment since orphanage directors seemed to live with the conscious or unconscious fear of a rebellion in their charges. The staffs were generally made up of individuals who were ill equipped to look after love-hungry children and were often incompetent, repressive individuals who denied individuality and family ties.[52]

The Orphan in Contemporary Western Culture

Before Freud, if sympathy were expressed at the death of a parent, it was offered to the surviving relatives who would be burdened with raising someone else's child. The orphan was told to be grateful for food, cloth-

---

50 Simpson, *Orphans.*
51 Magnuson & Petrie, *Orphan Train.*
52 Simpson, *Orphans.*

ing and shelter. An advertisement for insurance in America depicts how fragile a child's place was in the home, Figure 11.

Figure 11. Orphan asylum, An American Advertisement for the Prudential Insurance Company of America. Source: MPI/Archive Photos/Getty Images. Reprinted by permission.

It was not until the onset of World War II that therapists became interested in the experience of children who had lost their parents. In England, the government called upon Anna Freud to organize nurseries for infants whose fathers were sent away and whose mothers joined the work force. In 1945, she was asked to look after the survivors of concentration camps who had lost mother, father, relatives, homeland, and native language.

"At the third session of the Social Commission of the United Nations held in April 1948 it was decided to make a study of the needs of homeless children." The homeless were described as "children who are orphaned or separated from their families for other reasons and need care in foster homes, institutions or other types of group care."[53] This study, which was undertaken by John Bowlby in 1950, was to be confined to children who were homeless in their native country, thus excluding refugees from war or other disaster. He visited several countries in Europe, France, the Netherlands, Sweden, Switzerland, the United Kingdom, and the United States of America. As a result of his research of ordinary children, he believed that infants became attached to their mothers at six months. If the attachment were broken an infant would cry in protest hoping to bring the mother back. If she did not return, the protests turned into despair. According to Bowlby, while the child may continue to cry, more likely he or she[54] became withdrawn and made so little demand for attention that the adults looking after him or her mistook this phase as a sign that the distress had diminished. Moreover, the kind of attachment formed to the mother determined the emotional tone of future relationships developed throughout a person's life.

In the beginning of one's life, both the behavior of the caregiver and the behavior of the child are important. We now understand there needs to be the "good enough" fit between the mother and the child, and that there is a dialogue or relationship that must develop. Daniel Stern states, "all the events that regulate the feelings of attachment, physical proximity, and security are mutually created experiences…they cannot exist as part of known self-experience without an other."[55] While relationship is important in the beginning, it is also important as we grow and develop and encounter others on the journey. Jung described this in a seminar in March 1934:

---

53 J. Bowlby, *Child Care and the Growth of Love*, p. 7.
54 Attempts were made to use inclusive language of both sexes. However, at times I refrained in certain places from the constant repetition of using "he or she" in the text purely for the sake of readability.
55 D.N. Stern, *The Interpersonal World of the Infant*, p. 102.

And I told you in that connection that it was impossible for us to contain the whole of our psychology within ourselves; it is quite inevitable that certain parts will always be projected. That is the reason why we need other human beings, why we need objects; life makes no sense if completely detached, we are only complete in a community or in a relationship. There is no possibility of individuation on the top of Mount Everest where you are sure that nobody will ever bother you. Individuation always means relationship. Of course having a relationship does not mean that you are individuated, for relationship can also dismember you; you can be split into many parts, dissolved, if you don't hold onto yourself. But inasmuch as it forces you to cling to yourself, relationship is even the instigator of individuation. So collectivity is the worst poison if you dissolve in it; but if you can hold on to yourself while still keeping in touch with it, that is the ideal condition.[56]

Currently, there is a significant body of research on attachment and early development.[57] Significant is that any shortcoming of the mother's (parent's) empathic relation to the baby may lead to the beginning of an orphan complex.[58] Jacoby goes on to say that also an attitude of spoiling the child by fulfilling the slightest wishes may be harmful to meeting the child and his or her needs. The significance is the importance of the empathic attunement to the child's needs without interference of parental expectations for the child, which may be unconscious. Often one does not become aware of this until there is a behavioral manifestation, which is called to the attention of the parent generally by others outside

---

56 C. Douglas, *Visions: Notes of the Seminar Given in 1930-1934 by C.G. Jung*, p. 1367.

57 see: Ainsworth, 1967; Ainsworth, Blehar, Waters & Wall, 1978; Bowlby, 1960, 1965, 1980, 1982; Emde, 1983, 1988; Holmes, 1993; Karen, 1998; Klaus & Kennell, 1982; Lichtenberg, 1989; Shore, 1994, 1996, 1997a, 1997b, 2003; Srouf, 1989; Stern, 1985, 1995; Trevarthen, 1993; Wright, 1991; Zeanah & Boris, 2000.

58 Mario Jacoby, Personal communication, June 2, 2011.

of the immediate family constellation. This will be further discussed in
Chapter 3, The Psychological Orphan.

The Orphan in Contemporary Eastern Culture

In China, orphanages are no longer viewed as dumping grounds for
unwanted children[59] in contrast to earlier views documented in the
1990s.[60] During this time, those children who were frail and unrespon-
sive were not well attended to and essentially left to die as shown in
a 1995 British television documentary titled, *The Dying Room*.[61] Then
and now the majority of the orphans (usually abandoned children) were
female. Although current trends favor abortion, which has increased
with technological advances that can determine sex of the child *in utero*.
Traditionally, males in the Eastern culture carry on the family line and
provide financially for their parents in old age; girls marry and have
obligations to their husband's family. It is interesting to note that the
sex ratio for boys to girls is significantly higher in China, 119 boys to
100 girls, and India 115 boys to 100 girls, (USA has 105 boys to 100
girls births) and it is unclear where are the missing girls. I recall visiting
China in 1984 and seeing billboards promoting one child per family, a
time when the government began enforcing this rule, which was established in 1979. Now especially in rural areas in China, second births are
allowed, but it seems that the steep rise in sex differential between boys
and girls accounts for 70 percent of the missing girls, according to Eben-
stein of Harvard University.[62] In the 1990s this figure was reported to be
approximately 15 million girls.[63] The emotional plight of the child in an
orphanage is similar to the child in Western culture. Nevertheless, the
conditions of the hundreds of state-run orphanages in China continue
to be largely unknown.[64]

---

59 N. Chun, *Newsweek*.
60 T. Hilditch, *South China Morning Post*; A.F. Thurston, *The Atlantic
    Monthly*.
61 Chun, *Newsweek*.
62 J. Hsu, *Scientific American*.
63 Hilditch, *South China Morning Post*.
64 Chun, *Newsweek*.

India does not have a one-child policy, but due to cultural considerations and especially because girls were seen as financial burdens, the second and third births were more skewed towards male births. One inevitable consequence of this practice was that there will not be enough eligible women for the men to marry and so the men must seek partners in foreign countries.[65]

The emphasis on having children in homes with parents, rather than in orphanages, continues to be strong in the United States and the parentless or troubled youth are placed with foster parents. The Developing World countries continue to have orphanages and due to difficulties previously described by Bowlby, these children often have emotional scars making the adjustment to a new family in a new country difficult. Couples adopting children from other countries run the risk of acquiring a child with significant emotional problems. This has led to the employment by potential adopting parents of experts to help them weigh the risk of parenting a particular child before adoption. No longer are we in an age where we think love can cure all. And, at least in the United States, the support of the extended family has substantially diminished. The following story gives a glimpse of an orphan in contemporary Western culture.

An American Orphan Story

When we are following our destiny, the universe inevitably responds by presenting opportunities. The following interview came about by a friend, who knew of my interest in the orphan and introduced me to someone with whom he was working. This man told me he had been an orphan growing up. His story while poignant is however, not such an unusual story.

This middle-aged man, whom I shall call Adam, was born out of wedlock to a schizophrenic mother. The father, who did not live in the home, wanted to abort the pregnancy. Both were deemed "unfit parents" by social services and Adam was sent to live in a foster home at about age 4. His biological parents were physically abusive to him. As a

---

65 Hsu, *Scientific American.*

result of this abuse, Adam said he had "sore spots" by which he meant a vulnerability he continued to feel in relationship to others. He learned to cope, however, and now was employed full time, as well as, mentoring college-age youth who worked with him.

When he was about seven or eight he recalled there was a gang of boys who were going to beat up on him. Impulsively, Adam decided to select one of the boys to see if he could make him laugh. It worked and to his surprise the others stopped bothering him. As a result of being able to use humor, he realized that if others were in a good mood they would not hurt him. However, he sometimes overused the humor in interpersonal situations when it was not appropriate, including relationships within his family. He revealed that humor became his protection, stating, "The real me is vulnerable and scared."

Although he never remembered living with his biological family, he fantasized what the positive and negative aspects were of being in a family. From his perspective it didn't look like an advantage one way or another, because what he experienced were adults who were abusive, non-affirming and had no respect for children. This is an example of how vestiges of the way children were raised in previous times comes back to haunt us, especially when there is no empathic parent. As a teenager, Adam lived in an orphanage. There he learned to imitate any dialect, to fight well, and to communicate with people of other races. Next he went to a group home where he learned that there was no way to leave and find a new family and friends; he realized it would be like going from the known to the unknown which had the potential to be worse. For him he learned to "play by the rules" because then "you avoid the pitfalls."

When he began employment, he would tell others for whom he worked "Pay me what I'm worth." He worked hard and found a sense of belonging. He said, "I belonged to a tribe of workers," and because he had no connection to family this became his family. The values of truth and honesty became important to him despite an early encounter with his biological father who on a visit to see him tried to teach him to steal. Adam did not become a thief because his relationship experiences taught him about self-control and how to be with people. This needed sense of belonging far outweighed a temporary gain of material goods. As a result of his experiences he felt he could now survive any situation. This is the plight of the orphan, who has to rely on his own resourcefulness to survive.

Adam holds a responsible position as a craftsman. He views some of the disadvantaged youth who work for him as "bent trees," and he says some "you can't straighten out." However, he believes that if they can fight in their mind then they have a chance to make it.

For him, he realizes that "there is the person you show to the world and then there is the person that you really are, and when you become a survivalist, it is not who you really are." Adam who had married and had children told me, "I have a family, but I have none" which described the aloneness he feels. And he had to cut himself off from his true feelings early on because "I didn't want to see the demon in me." This is the terror that some orphans carry, the aloneness, the despair, and the insecurities, especially when there is no one with whom to share the experiences.

Chapter 3

THE PSYCHOLOGICAL ORPHAN

Those are the divine moments when something is clear and moving beyond the opposites and the suffering.

M-L von Franz[66]

The literal and historical orphan has been described, but what about those who experience feeling orphaned even though they are part of a family or network of friends and colleagues. Interestingly, there seems to be a prominence of orphans in the culture today. This appears to be a counterbalance of a materialistic world in which we can have it all, yes, but at what cost. We can have things that pretend to stave off aloneness, but often the materialistic and emotional needs are insatiable. We also live in a time in Western societies where we have become so busy that there is decreased time for personal interactions.

Just before the turn of the last century in Switzerland, the banks began charging for services rendered at the teller's window. This was to encourage people to use the automated technology, a people-less system, which is how many conduct their banking business for the sake of convenience. We have also turned to virtual relationships via the Internet and many people have "relationships" without actually meeting in person. These advances in technology can trigger the feeling of isolation,

66   M-L. von Franz, *Alchemy: An Introduction to the Symbolism and the Psychology*, p. 170.

which may be why we collect these electronic gadgets to attain the illusion of being connected. In turn, this may trigger the orphan complex, thus a feeling of being orphaned by these technological advances.

For those who have this feeling of being orphaned, something may be missing from early development; nevertheless, the feeling connects with the archetypal field, and certain conditions need to be there for this to happen. An archetypal experience is innate and is a structural element of the human psyche. The "archetypes are complexes of experiences that come upon us like fate and their effects are felt in our most personal life."[67]

Von Franz describes the collective unconscious as a field and "the excited points...would be called the archetypes,"[68] and this network of relationships among the many archetypes results in connections which manifest meaning. The orphan is not connected with this field of archetypal relationships. However, when the person is connected with these networks of relationships, the person with the orphan complex no longer feels so alone.

The archetypes have the potential for activation and are established *a priori* before birth. Jung states, "In early childhood a character is already there. You see a child is not born *tabula rasa* as one assumes. The child is born as a high complexity, with existing determinates that never waiver through the whole life,...."[69] Jung goes on to state that when a child has a neurosis he looks to see what is going on with the parents because the child is so much in the mental atmosphere of the parents. Because the child is in a *participation mystique* with the parents the child will express these influences in their childish way.

The historical context of attachment, and the more recent neurobiological research[70] suggest that patterns of interactions are set at a very early age through relationship to the primary caregivers. These patterns are predicated on the pre-symbolic organization of social interactions,

---

67   Jung, *Archetypes of the Collective Unconscious, CW 9i,* ¶ 62.

68   von Franz, *Alchemy,* p. 74.

69   R.I. Evans, *Conversations with Carl Jung and Reactions from Ernest Jones,* p. 34.

70   A.N. Schore, *Affect Regulation and the Origin of the Self: The Neurobiology of Emotional Development; Affect Regulation and the Repair of the Self.*

where organization means relatively persistent patterns or classifications of information.[71] The good news is that there is ongoing capacity for self-organization in the context of the interactive field throughout a person's lifetime, which highlights Jung's statements about the importance of relationship, an interaction with flexibility, thus ensuring changes that can happen over time.

Prior to this research, the work of Bowlby helped us to define attachment. Bowlby claimed that the child's tie to the mother "…is best conceived as the outcome of a number of instinctual response systems, mostly non-oral in character, which are part of the inherited behavior repertoire of man; when they are activated and the mother figure is available, attachment behavior results."[72] These patterns are evidenced by the infant crying and smiling which evoke maternal responses; and sucking, following and clinging, which the infant actively seeks and thus sustains contact and proximity with the caregiver. Lichtenberg paraphrases this to be conceived as "…patterns that make up an innate, preprogrammed motivational system."[73] He views these patterns as expressive of a motivational system activated in the infant and mother in whom attachment is a mutually regulatory experience that naturally results. However, as Main, Kaplan, and Cassidy[74] have suggested, the expectations for the other form a set of conscious and unconscious rules that guide appraisals of experience and behavior. However, this is not the whole story, because the archetype can arise spontaneously.

The importance of the attachment research emphasizes the experiences in one's life and how they may contribute to certain complexes, and of course, how they may be distressing for an individual. Mario Jacoby in his book, *Jungian Psychotherapy and Contemporary Infant Research*, states that archetypes are "…the basic species-specific dispositions which orga-

71   Beebe & Lachmann, *Infant Research and Adult Treatment Co-Constructing Interactions.*
72   J. Bowlby, *The Psychoanalytic Study of the Child*, p. 9.
73   J.D. Lichtenberg, *Psychoanalysis and Motivation*, p. 70.
74   Main, Kaplan & Cassidy, *Monographs of the Society for Research in Child Development.*

nize and regulate human behavior and experience."[75] Of course, these archetypal dispositions are interwoven with the environment, the temperament of the infant, and the reaction from the caregivers, and thus we find the origin of many complexes. Whether the infant experiences "good-enough" parenting or abandonment, these experiences will lay the foundation in the unconscious from which feeling-toned complexes originate.

Complexes are activated in confrontation with the world. As an infant, a set of expectancies is developed which Stern describes as "a structure indicating the likely course of events, based on averaged experiences."[76] According to Jacoby these "representations of interactions that have been generalized, RIGs" are the fantasies and expectations about interactions with significant others. These patterns of interactions are closely connected to complexes, and they can be positive, e.g., establishing a strong ego complex or negative, e.g., disturbing our sense of well-being and "interfering also with our capacity to relate to others and function the way we would like."[77]

In addition, Jung states that there may be autonomous complexes that come from the collective unconscious.[78] We often try to rationalize these problems in terms of external causes, but this may not be enough because the root of the matter may also lie within our psyche. Jung states[79]

> ...these experiences occur either when something so devastating happens to the individual that his whole previous attitude to life breaks down, or when for some reason the contents of the collective unconscious accumulate so much energy that they start influencing the conscious mind.

---

75 M. Jacoby, *Jungian Psychotherapy and Contemporary Modern Infant Research: Basic Patterns of Emotional Exchange*, p. 87.

76 Stern, *The Interpersonal World of the Infant*, p 97.

77 Jacoby, *Jungian Psychotherapy*, p. 93.

78 Jung, The Psychological Foundations of Belief in Spirits, *The Structure and Dynamics of the Psyche, CW 8*, ¶ 594.

79 Jung, Psychological Foundations, *Structure, CW 8*, ¶ 594.

Regardless of the complex by which one is touched, if we are stuck we need to find a way out. Portia Nelson[80] describes this in her book, *There's a Hole in My Sidewalk*.

Autobiography in 5 Short Chapters

Chapter I
I walk down the street.
There is a deep hole in the sidewalk
I fall in.
I am lost ... I am helpless.
It isn't my fault.
It takes forever to find a way out.

Chapter II
I walk down the same street.
There is a deep hole in the sidewalk.
I pretend I don't see it.
I fall in again.
I can't believe I am in the same place.
But, it isn't my fault.
It still takes a long time to get out.

Chapter III
I walk down the same street.
There is a deep hole in the sidewalk.
I *see* it is there.
I still fall in ... it's a habit ... but,
my eyes are open.
I know where I am.
It is *my* fault.
I get out immediately.

---

80 Nelson, *There's a Hole in My Sidewalk: The Romance of Self-Discovery*, pp. xi-xii.

Chapter IV
I walk down the same street.
There is a deep hole in the sidewalk.
I walk around it.

Chapter V
I walk down another street.

Easy to say but so hard to do! The importance of this poem is in the hope we acquire some consciousness over the years so that we do not continue to make the same mistakes. The challenging part is the acquisition of consciousness requiring patience, and of course, this is a lifetime process of which there are few simple formulas.

The Individual Way

In 1950, Jung published his work on the phenomenology of the self in *Aion*. Here he attempted to shed light on the change of the psychic situation within the Christian time, that is, over the past 2000 years. The writing came from his experience and from his experiences with patients. Jung's concern was that people were falling into a state of suggestibility, which he felt was the "...cause of Utopian mass-psychoses of our time."[81] By this it seemed that people were not thinking for themselves that is, not thinking independently; merely going along with the crowd.

In the first few chapters of *Aion*, Jung defines and expands on the ego, the shadow, the anima and animus and the Self. These concepts are important to understand for one's journey toward wholeness, toward finding one's unique way.

---

81 Jung, Forward, *Aion: Researches into the Phenomenology of the Self*, *CW 9ii*,
    p. x.

Ego

Jung describes the ego as:

> We understand the ego as the complex factor to which all
> conscious contents are related. It forms, as it were the centre
> of the field of consciousness; and, in so far as this comprises
> the empirical personality, the ego is the subject of all personal
> acts of consciousness.[82]

In order for one to be aware of something, it has to be conscious and
the ego is the center of consciousness, that is, all consciousness must go
through the ego in order for anything to be understood and even exist.
The idea that one exists, is conscious, came to Jung as early as about
eleven years old. He describes this in *Memories, Dreams, Reflections* as
emerging from a dense cloud and that things no longer merely happened to him, but that now he happened to himself; "…now I exist!"[83]
At this time, Jung had a vision as he walked to the cathedral square,
coming out of school at noon when children usually went home for
lunch. While he was admiring the cathedral and thinking of the beauty
of the church and how God had made this, a reprehensible thought
came into his mind with which he struggled for several days, trying to
make it go away. His mother noticed asking him if something had happened at school, which he denied. Finally he gathered his courage and
let the thought express itself.

> I saw before me the cathedral, the blue sky. God sits on His
> golden throne, high above the world—and from under the
> throne an enormous turd falls upon the sparkling new roof,
> shatters it, and breaks the walls of the cathedral asunder.[84]

Jung did not share this secret with anyone and he experienced an
"unendurable loneliness" wondering if others had similar experiences.

---

82 Jung, The Ego, *Aion: Researches into the Phenomenology of the Self, CW 9ii,
    CW, 9ii,* ¶ 1.
83 Jung, *MDR*, p. 44.
84 Jung, *MDR*, p. 50.

His mother later told him that during those days she thought he was depressed, but he thought it was more that he was brooding on the secret. Jung reasoned that everything came from God and it was His will that thoughts came into our awareness and thus it is "the miracle of grace which heals all and makes all comprehensible."[85] And he came to understand that while he lived in the present time there was also an "Other" in him that was "the timeless, imperishable stone."[86] An experience such as this can come when we are children as it did for Jung; sometimes there is a particular often painful event that ignites us to re-examine who we are.

This was the case for Sally, who presented with difficulties in being sexually intimate with her partner. She found this quite surprising and specifically wanted help to overcome this. She had been examined physically and found to have no medical reasons for her decreased sexual desire. After some discussion, it was revealed that she was ambivalent about marrying her fiancée and wanted a chance to live on her own since she had never experienced this. While he seemed like the perfect mate, something in her was not ready to make this kind of commitment and the symptom was the metaphor for her inability to connect with him on an intimate level. A deeper part of herself, an animus or mother or orphan complex was not ready to make this commitment. Of course, now she had a dilemma to face. Does she tell him this and risk losing the relationship? Would he understand? How can she be free to be her own person and still have a relationship with him? Can she risk being authentic? The answers were difficult and soul wrenching.

Shadow

Jung has defined the shadow as "the 'negative' side of the personality, the sum of all those unpleasant qualities we like to hide, together with the insufficiently developed functions."[87] We experience the shadow as projections onto another person of all the things we are not; he or she is

---

85 Jung, *MDR*, p. 51.
86 Jung, *MDR*, p. 53.
87 Jung, On the Psychology of the Unconscious, *Two Essays on Analytical Psychology*, CW 7, ¶ 103, n. 5.

"too fat," "lazy," "stubborn." It is these qualities that we have to look at and question, could this be a part of me? If it is, how can I withdraw the projections and relate more authentically to the individual on whom I have projected such a notion?

This is often seen in couples, where one partner will talk about the inadequacies of the other, and especially in couple's therapy where it is the other person who always needs to be fixed! I recall a couple in which the wife initiated the therapy saying the husband was always preoccupied and not available to the family for fun activities or vacations. It turned out the husband was trying to run a business and tend to all the extracurricular activities of the children taking them to school and their activities, while his wife was at work. She had little appreciation for the things he was doing and could only see the things he was not doing. It turned out that she had decreased energy for the family since the birth of their last child, which she did not want, and this was a way to avoid him and to be critical of him. This served the purpose of isolating them from a genuine relationship in which they could co-parent their children until each could be more aware of the anger and punishing attitude carried toward the other. When she could become conscious of this dynamic, withdraw the projection, then improvement in their relationship could occur.

The importance of the shadow is that we make these characteristics more conscious and this is often the first step in an analysis. To be aware that these characteristics are not simply bound to others, but that I, too, must be aware of how they exist within me in order to live more authentically.

Anima/Animus

If we think of the psyche as levels, with the ego being the most conscious, we then drop down from the shadow to the anima/animus. Jung talked about this in terms of syzygy, a yoking together of two aspects of the psyche, the masculine and the feminine. The anima is the feminine part of the man's psyche and the animus is the masculine part of the woman's psyche. The anima and animus act as a bridge to the Self, at a deeper level in the psyche. Jung says, the anima and animus are composed of three factors: the contra sexual qualities of the individual, the person's life experience of the opposite sex, and the archetypal image, which is innate.[88] Here the experiences with the mother and sisters for the man, and father and brothers for the woman, and lovers for both are very important. These, of course, connect with archetypes, which will be sources of inspiration or may be personifications of destiny or fate. Every archetype has two sides, a positive and a negative, and thus there may be suffering but it is through this suffering that we find the gold, the good, and the newfound awareness. One such connection can be made to the orphan.

A woman I knew was very much alone and had been married several times. Each marriage ended with the husband leaving her. She had loved each of these men, but was always betrayed and abandoned. It was a fate that was being lived out, in this case from her father who was unable to value her unique talents and would tell her how she needed to marry the doctor versus becoming one herself despite her good intellectual abilities. She did indeed do as her father wished, he only wanting the best for his daughter by marrying such men, but it always fell short because it denied her true nature. In addition, the father seemed to harbor a wish that his daughter would always be there for him. She felt so alone and the orphan archetype was activated in her, a personification of the fate she was living. This abandonment while painful was her opportunity to discover her own nature and potential. She was repeatedly being thrown back onto herself to discover her own and unique meaning of her life. And this is what happens, we are continually faced with challenging issues until we become conscious of their meaning.

There are several possibilities for the anima/animus connection. The first is the state whereby one is in love and has found their soul mate, but predictably this state cannot last forever. Another state is when the projections on the partner are withdrawn, and perhaps directed toward another, affairs for example, but this produces pain and abandonment and often times rage in the partner. Another possibility is for the projections to be withdrawn from the other and a realization that each has carried these projections, which now being withdrawn can lead to the

---

88 Jung, The syzygy: Anima and animus, *Aion*, *CW, 9ii*, ¶ 41, fn 5.

discovery of and the capacity for conscious love. This is the couple that can love the partner for who he or she actually is, while developing and maintaining a relationship to the inner image of the anima or animus within. This is the difficult part of love, to accept the other, as they are, not for who we want them to be, and to be understanding of the other which requires a mutual understanding of honoring one's own individual way.

Kathy was a 39-year-old woman who had been in a marriage about 10 years and was generally unsatisfied in the relationship. Her husband was also not very responsible with the finances and she found herself nagging and directing him. They decided to separate, but he remained a good father and companion to his wife. However, she continued to bemoan that he should show more responsibility and initiate marital counseling as a sign of his love and commitment to her. He continued to be passive in his relationship to her, longing for the mother he had lost at an early age; he desired to be taken care of, and she feared to be more intimate anticipating rejection and abandonment, which was the experience she had with her father. However, these wishes only maintained the status quo. She was reluctant to withdraw her projections and move toward having more intimacy with him for fear of being disappointed that he would not be responsive to her. He was intimidated by her competence, which did not allow him to have a voice. Because they could not withdraw their projections, nothing changed and both remained stuck. Both were fearful of initiating the step of showing commitment and discovering the potential for intimacy, regardless if they decided to stay together or not.

The fear of intimacy is real because it is like facing someone in all of one's nakedness, and as Clarissa Pinkola Estes states, in order to live with the most feeling, "…one must go up against the very thing one fears most." [89] She likens it to sleeping with Lady Death because in love there are many beginnings and endings if one has the bravery to endure and a "…heart that is willing to die and be born and die and be born again and again."[90] Therefore, deep love requires the death of the ego;

89 C.P. Estes, *Women Who Run With the Wolves: Myths and Stories of the Wild Woman Archetype*, p. 131.
90 Estes, *Women Who Run With the Wolves*, p. 149.

the death of everything one believes to be and to, thus, is emotionally naked before the other.

As a scientist, Jung emphasized the importance of one's experience, because it is the only encounter we have and here is where the healing begins no matter what the source. In order to do this, we must use the experience as our teacher and learn what we must from the situation.

Self

At the deepest level is the Self, a rather complex term, which is only possible to understand from various angles.[91] In one of his last writings, Jung suggested calling the total personality the Self.[92] Previously, Jung described the Self as follows: "The Self is not only the centre, but also the whole circumference, which embraces both conscious and unconscious; it is the centre of this totality, just as the ego is the centre of consciousness."[93] This may be a bit confusing because one has to differentiate the ego from the Self. That is, the ego is consciousness, it is what I know subjectively, and it is borne from the Self. The Self is what is known objectively; the Self includes the experienceable and the not yet experienced.[94]

We see the Self manifest in dreams, myths and fairytales where it appears as an extraordinary personality, "supraordinate personality" according to Jung.[95] In the development of the ego, we know that the ego emerges from the Self, that is, we develop more awareness as we grow, learn the rules of society and learn to function adequately. However, the danger is that we equate the ego and the Self, and it is important to note there are differences. Jung talks about this in terms of a duality and for him this was apparent when he became aware of personality one and personality two within himself.[96] The hypothetical ideal is when there is

---

91 Edinger, *The Aion Lectures: Exploring the Self in C.G. Jung's Aion.*
92 Jung, The Ego, *Aion, CW, 9ii*, ¶ 9.
93 Jung, Individual Dream Symbolism in Relation to Alchemy, *Psychology and Alchemy, CW 12*, ¶ 44.
94 Jung, Definitions, *Psychological Types, CW 6*, ¶ 789.
95 Jung, *Psychological Types, CW 6*, ¶ 790.
96 Jung, *MDR*, pp. 92-95.

no ego-Self identity, and then we can act from our psychological center with more consciousness and awareness and genuine authenticity.

The importance of these concepts form the theme of this book, that is, when one becomes identified with an archetype, in this case the orphan, one acts and sets up the world as if this is the only truth. In the second half of life, we have the potential for the perspective that we no longer need to be tied to such an archetype or any archetype for that matter. The archetype may have been with us for a time, but we no longer need to identify with it. However the ego, regardless if this identification has been positive or negative, will hold on until some consciousness can develop, and then the ego can relinquish control and become in partnership with the Self.

This change comes with the gift of the symbol in forms of images of wholeness from the unconscious. According to Jung,[97] "although wholeness seems at first sight to be nothing but an abstract idea, it is nevertheless empirical in so far as it is anticipated by the psyche in the form of spontaneous or autonomous symbols." More or less the real meaning of symbol production "…is to bring to all men and…therefore lead the individual out of his isolation."[98] In the German version of C.G. Jung's *The Collected Works*, this passage, the word "*vereinzelung*" is used which has been translated in the English version as isolation. However, the meaning goes beyond this, not only to come out of isolation, but to overcome or go beyond a separate existence as the orphan.[99] How might we envision such a journey?

The Alchemy of the Orphan

Jung talked about how the early ancestors imbued everything with psychic meaning and hidden connections with transpersonal powers. These early ancestors, like the child, lived in a world that was continuous with oneself, and therefore one was not alone. For Jung, the inner and outer lives have a meaning and are expressions of transpersonal patterns and

97 Jung, The Self, *Aion, Researches Into the Phenomenology of the Self, CW, 9ii,* ¶ 59.
98 Jung, The Philosophical Tree, *Alchemical Studies, CW 13,* ¶ 396.
99 Schweizer, Personal communication, September 5, 2012.

powers.[100] For the person who is in connection with the Self, there is no such thing as chance; everything that happens has a meaning and there is a spiritual connection, and again one is not alone.

Thus, in the early stages of psychological development, "God," the highest value, is hidden in the identification with or projected into the external world. We tend to think everything emanates from our own thoughts. This idea of the hidden God corresponds to the Gnostic myth of Sophia, who is the divine (female) wisdom in Latin, *sapientia*. In the process of creation, Sophia became lost and imprisoned in matter becoming the hidden God or Goddess, which was in need of release and redemption. This is an image for the highest value that is hidden in identification with matter, that is, a physical substance as distinct from mind and spirit. Therefore, Sophia or wisdom needs to be released through the alchemical process, a process by which ordinary materials are made into precious ones, a metaphor for the task of developing consciousness.

This theme of the redemption of God was basic to alchemy. In the symbolic language of the alchemists, the orphan was an image for the Philosophers' Stone, *Lapis Philosophorum*, that dissolves, that is, dies, in order to allow God to arise from the dead.[101] The connection is that the orphan was an image for the magic 'stone' to melt and dissolve to bring about the transformation of the lead into gold. The stone was produced from *materia prima* by complex processes, which were supposed to transform nonprecious metals into precious ones, thereby rejuvenating and healing. In these processes, the separation and rejoining of opposing principles, especially the masculine and feminine, played an important role, which is why the Philosophers' Stone was also frequently depicted as a Hermaphrodite.[102] (see Figure 12 next page.)

---

100   Edinger, *Ego and Archetype*.
101   U. Becker, *The Element Encyclopedia of Symbols*.
102   Jung, *Alchemical Studies, CW 13*, p. 152 B2.

Figure 12. The filius or rex in the form of a Hermaphrodite.
Source: Jung, 1942, p. 152 B2.

Moreover, to submit the material to the alchemical process means to apply conscious effort and attention to this process. The goal is to freely access the Self without the constraints from the ego. All critical attempts to discover the meaning of the Philosophers' Stone have been interpreted by some more advanced alchemists such as Dorn and Khunrat as symbolic actions that were basically visible accompaniments of psychologically and religiously motivated transformation processes. That is, by a sort of death, the originally formless *prima materia* decomposes into its constituent elements and achieves a resurrection on a higher level – to a level of increased consciousness. Jung[103] has interpreted these

103 Jung, Paracelsus as a Spiritual Phenomenon, *Alchemical Studies, CW 13*, ¶ 185.

actions as related to the individuation process; the journey one takes toward wholeness.

> By means of the 'thousand fold distillation' they hoped to achieve a particularly 'refined' result. ...this was not an ordinary chemical operation, it was essentially a psychological procedure. The fire to be used was a symbolical fire, and the distillation had to start from the 'midst of the centre' (*ex medio centri*).

Jung speaks about the contrast between the Christian attitude, by which humankind with a passive attitude achieves redemption through faith, and the alchemical attitude, which is an active effort in man to redeem God.

In the Christian formulation, "...man attributes the need of redemption to himself and leaves the work of redemption, the actual ἆθλον or *opus,* to the autonomous divine figure."[104] In the alchemical formulation, "man takes upon himself the duty of carrying out the redeeming *opus,* and attributes the state of suffering and consequent need of redemption to the *anima mundi* imprisoned in matter."[105]

When one realizes the reality of the connection within the ego – Self axis, then the process of individuation has the potential to unfold. The center is no longer the ego, but the connection between the ego and the Self is paramount; thus the dialogue of individuation is not possible as long as the ego thinks that everything in the psyche is of its own making.[106] Being in connection with the Self in alchemical terms, allows for something new to develop, a creativity that was not there before; it is really something totally new. This can be applied to the orphan because when one stands alone then one has the potential for uniqueness. When we speak of the orphan symbolically, the orphan, who is alone and solitary, has the potential to be on the path toward individuation toward becoming a unique individual.

---

104 Jung, Religious Ideas in Alchemy, *Psychology and Alchemy, CW 12,* ¶ 414.
105 Jung, Religious Ideas, *Psychology and Alchemy, CW 12,* ¶ 414.
106 Edinger, *Ego and Archetype,* p. 103.

The Oxherder

In the Buddhist tradition, there is a parable that has some meaning for the discovery of finding the way. The Oxherder, a Zen parable text, first appeared in the present form as drawn by the Chinese Zen master Kaku-an Shien in the Sung dynasty (960-1279).[107] Traditional Buddhism has its origins in India, where it evolved from the life and teachings of Siddhartha.

The entire parable is detailed in *Buddhism and Jungian Psychology* by Spiegelman and Miyuki, however the story has implications for the individual journey. The Eastern tradition would emphasize meditation and mindlessness while the Western tradition would emphasize imagination and discrimination. However, both traditions emerge with "clarity, serenity, joy, ego-lessness...."[108] Keep in mind that as long as one lives in a mortal body, then the losing and finding of the ox, one's way, will occur again and again.

The concept behind the oxherding story can be compared to an early sutra comparing the herding of cattle to the responsibilities of a Buddhist monk.[109] The story most likely evolved out of China, where the image of the ox has religious significance as a fertility symbol, associated with agriculture and the prevention of floods and natural disasters.[110] Wada goes on to say that in Daoist philosophy, the ox and the herdboy were representative of the seasonal rhythms of nature suggesting a feminine symbol even though no female figures are in the story. The significance is not whether there are males or females depicted, but rather the presence of the masculine and feminine. This highlights the growth and differentiation of the archetypal opposites and not solely development of the ego. Therefore, there is "...the need to civilize and differentiate as well as to redeem and recover our origins in nature and instinct."[111]

The poem describes the seeker's progression toward enlightenment portrayed in a series of ten pictures. In the West we can also think of

107 Spiegelman & Miyuki, *Buddhism and Jungian Psychology*.
108 Spiegelman & Miyuki, *Buddhism and Jungian Psychology*, p. 74.
109 D.T. Suzuki, *Essays in Zen Buddhism*.
110 S. Wada, *The Oxherder: A Zen Parable Illustrated*.
111 Spiegelman & Miyuki, *Buddhism and Jungian Psychology*, p. 50.

this like an individuation process. The story begins with a herdboy who becomes separated from his ox and then sets out to find the animal. Initially, he is confused by intersecting mountain paths; he is far from home and exhausted from his efforts and assailed by feelings of doubt. He notices traces of the missing ox, but cannot distinguish truth from falsehood. In the third picture he hears the sound of the ox and when all his senses are working together his eyes are opened and he catches the first glimpse of the ox's head. The ox has been alone for a while and has become wild and is difficult to catch. The boy catches it, but the ox is stubborn and resists, he must persevere and use a whip. In the fifth picture, he holds the nose-rope tightly and the ox is finally calmed; he keeps a firm grip and he is able to control the ox. He realizes that delusion is something that originates within himself, not in the world around him.

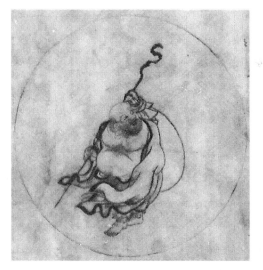

Figure 13. Hotei. Source: Stephanie Wada,[112]
Mary & Jackson Burke Foundation. Reprinted by permission.

Finally having tamed the ox, the boy rides the ox towards home; his mind is clear and he does not look back. In picture seven the boy is back home, but the ox is no longer seen. The thought is that the boy now sees the truth and no longer needs what he was searching for and all confu-

112 Wada, *The Oxherder*, pp. 40-41.

sion is gone. The next picture is of the empty circle (ensō) where the ox and the herdboy are gone; emptiness remains suggesting there is no attachment to the self and earthly things. The next picture is an earthly scene with water, mountains, and flowers suggesting that the physical world has been transcended and one can observe that world from the vantage point of nonbeing. In the last picture, the herdboy is in the form of a Buddha-like figure, an enlightened being, an old man who is going to market. The figure is an old man suggesting the journey takes time (Figure 13).

This man has forgotten his own enlightenment and so here is the collective man who goes to market with his pupil and his beggar's bowl, and has even forgotten his experience with the Gods.[113] This means that he no longer feels unique, that is, this is not intentionally on his mind. Rather uniqueness springs from him as a creative act[114] and this is seen as the cherry trees blossom when he passes by them. The enlightened one does not feel unique, but feels very human, open to the world, and very human with everybody.

Such is the journey and as previously mentioned the losing and the finding of the ox will occur perhaps many times throughout a lifetime. Miyuki,[115] speaks of this journey as one in which the ego undergoes a relativization. Von Franz[116] states, "The ego must have the attitude of a human being among other human beings, and then the uniqueness, of it has been found within, will emanate involuntarily." Jung speaks of this in *Mysterium Coniunctionis*[117] giving as an example the King who has grown old but does not know this, that is, he is unconscious to the fact he is aging and no longer able to rule with the creativity and vigor of a more youthful person. He has no conscious knowledge that a new leader is needed. Thus, the old principle needs to die, that is, the old habits and opinions have to die in order to make space for something new.

---

113   von Franz, *Alchemy*.
114   von Franz, *Alchemy*.
115   Spiegelman & Miyuki, *Buddhism and Jungian Psychology*.
116   von Franz, *Alchemy*, p. 160.
117   Jung, Rex and Regina, *Mysterium Coniunctionis*, CW 14, ¶ 368.

James was a 75-year old man who wanted to live to be 120 and was determined to live his life to the fullest. However, he was in a co-dependent relationship with his wife and often felt hampered in doing things independent from her. She constantly worried about him because he would leave the house and take hikes without telling anyone where he was going or he would spontaneously do things and forget to tell her his whereabouts. Recently, he wanted to kayak and to negotiate this agreed to consult his physician, who stated he was in good health and approved he could participate in this activity. James wanted to participate in the outer world at a time in his life when he needed a new approach to the inner world. He will find a solution to living out the rest of his life if he can have more reflection on the inner world and his unique spirituality. This may be a spiritualization of "matter." That is, external events through which he was trying to find meaning and yet yielded little satisfaction. From the kayaking experience he began to become more conscious of the importance of leading his life authentically and as an individual separate from his wife. Once he realized this the activity of kayaking held less value.

In order to become conscious the ego and its contents must assume a relative position to a standpoint outside of itself. This can come through archetypal or numinous dream images or shadow work, in which one gains a larger perspective. And the ego then becomes relative to the whole psyche. An example for James was the following dream during this time:

> My wife and I are going to a national church meeting that includes lay and clergy. My wife buys a *People* magazine and has it with her. The high church officials are banishing everyone who will attend this meeting, but I am still going to go.

His wife in reality has a point, that is, as one ages precautions need to be taken into account. However, for this couple he needed to take more of a spiritual stance befitting him and not the collective voice that his wife carried in the dream. His associations to this dream were of Jesus healing the blind man and his parents then got kicked out of the synagogue. For him it was the importance of taking a stand even if one was against the masses and that it was worse to not see when one's eyes are opened. His work was to focus on the inner spiritual development and to find a way to peaceful contentment with his wife in a less dependent relationship.

The journey is a solitary one, in which one learns to accept oneself for what one is and to be comfortable enough with oneself to accept this in others; to accept them for what they are regardless of their position in life. It is a journey, according to the oxherder story, in which there is nothing to know, no ultimate universal truth. Suzuki[118] reflects, "…when one sees into the inmost of one's own being, one instantly becomes a Buddha…."

The Individual Journey

Angela was a divorced woman currently entering her senior years who had a childhood dream at age 10 that she could never forget. This was the dream:

> I am in a desert, crawling on my hands and knees. The sand has a red-like color to it and the landscape is barren; no vegetation only mountains in the distance. It is scorching hot and the sun is bearing down on me. I am very thirsty and struggling to find water. I wake up sweating.

Let's look at the dream and try to understand what this might be about for her. Childhood dreams, according to Jung[119] "…are of the utmost importance because they are dreamed out of the depth of the personality and, therefore, frequently represent an anticipation of the later destiny." This was a dream she could not forget and had stayed with her a long time suggesting, the dream held a particular significance for her.

This dream came at the time when she was being exposed to sexuality through education at school, was beginning to enter puberty and was noting her bodily changes. She recalled feeling somewhat destabilized by this information regarding sexuality and what it would mean for her. She

118 Suzuki, *Essays in Zen Buddhism*, p. 363.
119 Jung, *Children's Dreams: Notes from the Seminar Given in 1936-1940 by C.G. Jung*, p. 1.

was particularly close with her father and did not like the stay-at-home qualities of what was modeled by her mother.

The dream begins in the desert, which while not as barren as that described in the dream, was the family's place of residence. She recalls moving there a few years previously and having to leave a male childhood friend behind. This was devastating for her such that she refused to participate in her new classroom and make friends and showed a lot of anger at her parents, who had tried to prepare her, but somehow neither she nor her parents realized or anticipated the loss she would suffer. The loss of her childhood friend was difficult because they were very close and enjoyed having adventures while playing together, visiting one another's homes frequently. This loss also became a destiny. The desert seemed to exaggerate her experience of desolation and loneliness. Thus, she experienced too much yang (the active male principle of the universe) qualities, fire, sun, masculine and aggressive, and lack of the yin (the passive female principle of the universe) qualities of water, feminine and flexibility. Yang-yin refers to the light and dark, which have come to be extended to include the two polar forces of the universe and the cycle of change.[120]

The desert on the other hand can be a place where plants and animals survive and thrive on very little. As a psychic landscape, the desert may portray "...periods of alienation, spiritual thirst and creative tedium, disorientation and depletion, and also mortification, purification, redemption and initiation." According to these editors, the desert was a transitional space of wandering, exile, temptation and waiting for promise in the Bible.[121] Thus, the desert is a place of trial and also a place of encounter.

In Egypt the desert was ruled over by the god Set and it was where the cat goddess Bastet became the lioness Sekhmet. Von Franz tells us that the lion goddess, Skemet, and the cat goddess, Bastet, were intertwined with Isis in the late Egyptian tradition. Bastet as the daughter of Isis and her husband Osiris, was known as the Lady of Bubastis and there was a temple for her in the center of town surrounded by water.[122]

120 *I Ching*.
121 Ronnberg & Martin, *The Book of Symbols*, p. 116.
122 von Franz, *The Cat: A Tale of Feminine Redemption*.

Bastet and Isis contained both the higher spirituality and also the darker chthonic aspects of the Great Mother.

Bastet was at times identified with her father and took a place among the solar heroes of all mythology that fight with the devil. Bastet was worshipped as lunar because of its reflecting eyes, just as the light of the sun is reflected in the moon. Bastet was also linked with fertility and hence all creative processes. Thus, we have a feminine consciousness, and this dream may point to a needed development in the feminine consciousness.

Sekhmet, who is portrayed on Egyptian tombs as recounted in *The Sungod's Journey to the Netherworld*, embodies the ambivalence of all life.[123] She is known to cause illness, but also to cause the healing and it is in the healing that the feminine is present.

In the dream Angela was close to the earth, crawling on her hands and knees and at a more primitive state of seeking a connection to the archetypal mother and perhaps a needed departure from the personal mother who she experienced as emotionally unavailable. The sun is bearing down on her and there is hardship in her life of which she cannot yet understand the meaning. It is a predominately male orientation or striving for consciousness that causes the terrible thirst from which she could die. This is a too one-sided connection to the masculine values in her life, and a lack of feminine containing and nurturing.

Angela was an only child and she had wanted siblings, but her parents were older and did not want more children. She longed for companions, and so joined organizations and clubs to create a sense of family for herself. However, despite belonging to these organizations she still felt alone much of the time. The archetype of the orphan, being alone in the desert, had been activated within her even at this early age and it was played out in her life. Her father died when she was in her early 20s and she was devastated by this loss and so married shortly after his death to fill the void. That marriage did not last.

Angela lost a significant companion in her childhood friend with whom she could share her love and then again in her father approxi-

---

123 A. Schweizer, *The Sungod's Journey Through the Netherworld: Reading the Ancient Egyptian Amudat.*

mately 10 years later. She then sought out to replace these figures, but it was never satisfactory and the orphan was constellated over and over again.

The color in her dream is reminiscent of the renewing or destroying aspects of red as in blood and fire, which can bring life or destruction, insight, love or aggression.[124] The red sand color is seen in the paintings of Georgia O'Keefe who found her creative inspirations in the deserts of New Mexico where she was able to flourish and be creative. Her first glimpse of the Sangre de Cristo Mountains inspired paintings; she loved the landscapes there, but was not able to return for another 12 years.[125] Red is often associated with Seth as the opponent of White Horus and Black Osiris and the ship of the king in Egypt was painted red to suggest Seth was made a slave to carry the sun.[126] Horus and Seth were opponents in the Osiris myth and destined to fight until they finally reconcile and ally with each other, gaining their own rights. This was symbolized in the double-headed figure of the sungod in which was personified the union of opposites, the two faces of everything that exists.[127]

The uniting of opposites is taken up by Jung in 'The Personification of the Opposites,' *Mysterium Coniunctionis*[128] in which he states, "The alchemist's endeavors to unite the opposites culminate in…the supreme act of union in which the work reaches its consummation." Specifically this was an attempt by the alchemists to unite the opposites in matter, to unite Sol (Sun) and Luna (Moon). Regarding the red, Sol contains an active sulfur of a red color that is hot and dry, perhaps, reflected in the red sand. In her dream Angela suffers from an aggressive aspect of the dark Sun (*Sol niger*) which signals one to do something. Thus, the image of the hot sun and red sand can be seen as a positive creative force to return to the *prima materia* in order "…to get back to the original

---

124   Abt, *Introduction to Picture Interpretation: According to C.G. Jung.*

125   M. Costantino, *Georgia O'Keefe.*

126   deVries, *Dictionary of Symbols and Imagery.*

127   Schweizer, *Sungod's Journey.*

128   Jung, The Personification of the Opposites, *Mysterium Coniunctionis, CW 14,* ¶ 104.

condition of the simple elements and attain the incorrupt nature of the pre-worldly paradise":[129] a potential for healing.

The dark side of the sun is connected with the father, since he is the first carrier of the animus image for a woman. Angela took on a rather rigidly, righteous character in her early school years and would make sure the teacher knew of all the minor infractions in which other students were engaging. This was later followed in adolescence by acting out against the rules.

"Psychologically, Seth symbolizes an instinctive, sometimes even violent aspect of the self, that is, of any realization of one's own innermost truth…[which] is indispensable for the process of individuation."[130] Seth embodies the shadow aspects and the dark impulses and perhaps frightening qualities. This energy is needed for a moral-ethical differentiation of the individual, and for the person to take new responsibility. To accept the Seth-like qualities we all have would be to integrate these shadow aspects, those dark angry aspects within all of us, and also know that these qualities can be helpful and supportive.

The feminine as represented by Isis is the goddess of life and "…she is the great healer and protectress of all who are helpless and afflicted with disease, pain, and sorrow."[131] At times we feel stuck and this is because there has been no movement. The feminine has the potential to start the flow and encourage a development. The feminine is important because it is the holding, the patience, at times the passive waiting, and the loving kindness toward oneself that one needs to have to embark on such a journey. Sometimes one has to wait. The masculine, ego-driven, completing tasks are no longer helpful especially at the exclusion of the connection to the Self.

The desert, of course, can be real or imagined, and regardless one has to face the meaning for oneself. St. Anthony was known to have hungered in the desert, and the legend goes that he was fed by a raven, which is the emblem of the unforeseen sustenance in the psyche activat-

---

129 Jung, The personification of the opposites, *Mysterium Coniunctionis, CW 14,* ¶ 118.
130 Schweizer, *Sungod's Journey*, p. 142.
131 Schweizer, *Sungod's Journey*, p. 143.

ed by extremity.[132] The suggestion is that one must look and listen and detect the unique and unnoticed signs of life that exist in the desert, the water that is stored in the cactus, and know there are hidden resources within each of us.

Angela had lived a life in which she was over identified with the orphan, stuck in the desert. This was not realized for many years, until through Jungian analysis she slowly began to face the meaning of being alone. She had achieved in the outer world but had betrayed her own body in service of the masculine and neglected her intuitions for creative expression. Her journey was a long one and in the dream there was no water, but now she had an opportunity with her new found awareness to be in touch with the water of life. Of course, this journey was not an easy one, because she must become playful with her creativity and engage herself with the outer and inner world to inspire the creative spirit within the unconscious. As Schweizer[133] states, "Behind this phenomenon lies the principle of synchronicity, the probability that such playful, semiconscious activity will suddenly hit upon an archetypal content that is constellated in the unconscious." In Jung's discussion about synchronicity in "Synchronicity: An acausal connecting principle,"[134] he describes how a meaningful coincidence will surface and become the creative solution. Thus, the synchronistic event exists from all eternity and repeats itself sporadically and is mysterious. This is to what we must be open to receiving.

For Angela, as for all "victims" of the orphan complex, she must discover the flow of life. Too much heat, yang, sun, consciousness, firmness, must be balanced with yin, coldness, moon, unconsciousness and flexibility. The negative side is the dreadful isolation as we saw in Angela. On the positive side within the orphan complex, one has the potential to find his or her own uniqueness.

---

132 Ronnberg & Martin, *The Book of Symbols.*
133 Schweizer, *Sungod's Journey*, p. 144.
134 Jung, Synchronicity: An Acausal Connecting Principle, *The Structure and Dynamics of the Psyche, CW 8.*

Chapter 4

THE ORPHAN AS A SYMBOL

The Guest House

This being human is a guest house.
Every morning a new arrival.

A joy, a depression, a meanness,
some momentary awareness comes
as an unexpected visitor.

Welcome and entertain them all!
Even if they are a crowd of sorrows,
who violently sweep your house
empty of its furniture,
still, treat each guest honorably.
He may be clearing you out
for some new delight.

The dark thought, the shame, the malice,
meet them at the door laughing and invite them in.
Be grateful for whatever comes,
because each has been sent
as a guide from beyond.

J. Rumi[135]

---

135   J. Rumi, *The Essential Rumi*, p. 109.

The orphan touches us so deeply because of its archetypal nature. That is, like the divine child, the orphan is a universal experience known to us all. This is in contrast to the developmentally empathic failures of the parents' relationship with the child, specifically the empathic attunement. In the photographs of orphaned animals and homeless children, there is something that tugs at us to respond (Figures 14 & 15, Orphan Lamb and Soldier Feeds Cat).

Figure 14. Orphan, A Cumberland farmer bottle feeds an orphan lamb. Source: Hulton Archive/Fox Photos/Getty Images. Reprinted by permission.

Figure 15. Soldier Feeds Cat, A US Marine feeds an orphan kitten
found after heavy mortar barrage near "Bunker Hill" during the
Korean War. Source: Hulton Archive/Sgt Martin Riley/Getty
Images. Reprinted by permission.

In addition, note the photo of the innocent child in Figure 16.

Figure 16. The Infant Samuel. Source: Bridgeman Art Library.
Reprinted by permission.

It makes one think of the child who is not world-weary, who is full of life and hope for the future. There is the child who plays with the animals and who seems close to the instincts, to his or her instinctual nature. This child has hope and future and this seems to be what connects us to the archetype of the child. Let us consider how and why the orphan touches us and what are the implications.

To begin, the orphan is usually seen as a child and the divine child is a manifestation of the child archetype as seen in Jungian psychology. That the archetype is "divine" (or to the contrary "demonic") suggests that the archetype has been activated due to the affective reactions, which organize the conscious material in an archetypal way. Therefore, we need to understand the potential that the archetype holds for us. As previously noted, there have been children in myths and fairy tales that have had significant impact and the power to captivate.

Jung described the archetype as "typical modes of apprehension,"[136] that is, "as *a priori* conditioning factors . . . which gives all living organisms their specific qualities"[137]; he conceptualized an archetype to be a universal, primordial experience of humankind. The archetypal structures and patterns are, thus, a crystallization of experiences over centuries of time. He viewed them as connected to the instincts, "the collective unconscious consists of the sum of the instincts and their correlates, the archetypes."[138] This means that archetypes can be connected to instincts as well as to the spirit or a combination of both, but they remain in the collective unconscious to which we never have direct access. "The archetype is a tendency to form such representations of a motif—representations that can vary a great deal in detail without losing their basic pattern."[139] The orphan is one of those basic patterns.

The orphan archetype, and all archetypes for that matter, has a power. This is because the image of the child produces an impact, which has tremendous energy usually with a feeling of mystery, such that we are unable to remain unaffected. Here one must distinguish between the archetype and the archetypal image. It is "only when the archetypes come into contact with the conscious mind . . . can the conscious mind differentiate them.... Only then can consciousness apprehend, under-

---

136   Jung, The Structure of the Psyche, *The Structure and Dynamics of the Psyche, CW, 8,* ¶ 280.

137   Jung, A Psychological Approach to the Dogma of the Trinity, *Psychology and Religion, CW 11,* ¶ 222fn.

138   Jung, Structure, *Structure and Dynamics, CW 8,* ¶ 281.

139   Jung, von Franz, Henderson, Jacobi & Jaffe, *Man and His Symbols,* p. 67.

stand, elaborate, and assimilate them."[140] This is when we have an image that can be understood.

The emergence of an archetype must come from an individual experience, but it does not necessarily mean that it has to emerge from a personal event like an abuse or abandonment by one's parents or a significant person in one's life. "The archetype can emerge from an inner psychic event which then activates the complex and creates the respective archetypal image. I would even say that the real reason for many traumatic experiences is to be found in an inner psychic experience in the revelation or experience of the dark side of god, as it were."[141]

One place where images are activated is through sandplay therapy, a treatment modality developed by Dora Kalff and founded as the International Society for Sandplay Therapy (ISST) in 1985.[142] The basic elements of sandplay therapy are that the therapist provides a free and protected space: the client can select, usually from hundreds of miniatures, and make scenes in either a wet or a dry sand tray, or can simply mold the sand into shapes. It is a unique method for accessing the healing energies of the unconscious in which the psyche knows what is needed. Her work is derived from Margaret Lowenfeld, D. Suzuki and C.G. Jung. It was a technique that the following person utilized in her journey to healing, and one, which was used by a child later described in Chapter 6.

Anne was a 48-year-old professional woman who now found herself alone after a divorce she did not want. She tried for several years to hold on to the marriage, but despite her attempts at reconciliation, her husband was not willing to undertake the effort this would require. They had been a childless couple and shortly after the separation, they were finally selected by a young unwed mother to adopt her child. Anne thought this was the answer to her prayers—a literal divine child—had appeared. However, the husband did not see it the same way and was not willing to participate in raising a child or to reconcile with her. This threw Anne into a major depression for somehow she knew it would not be fair to adopt the child under these circumstances, and she was

140   J. Jacobi, *Complex/Archetype/Symbol in the Psychology of C.G. Jung*, p. 66.
141   Schweizer, Personal communication, September 9, 2010.
142   Mitchell & Friedman, *Sandplay: Past, Present and Future.*

in no shape to give emotionally to an infant. In addition, her career no longer brought her the satisfaction it once did and so she began an analysis. After a few years of this work, and having gained some perspective, she sought to reconnect to her creativity through sandplay therapy, and it was through this modality she discovered she was on a journey to find herself. And as a person alone, and even without parents now, the orphan within her was activated.

In Anne's situation adopting a child could not be a reality for her and so the divine child was a symbol, which needed further understanding. Of course, she mourned and felt the pain of the potential of never being a mother to her own child. She longed for the easy answer, but the answer had to come from within her, which became her journey of self-discovery. How often we want an answer that does not require any suffering, but every ounce of consciousness is a fight with the unconscious that entails suffering.

The Divine Child

The divine child is a symbol, not a human child. It is a symbol of a wonder-child, a child who is brought up in extraordinary circumstances. "Its deeds are as miraculous or monstrous as its nature and physical constitution."[143] In Jungian psychology, the divine child is not something that existed in the past, that is, that belongs to the collective unconscious but something that exists now. It is a symbol for renewal and hope that comes through our needs for compensation to a lost energy or creativity. Thus, the divine child becomes a symbol for a potential development.

As a symbol for a potential development, "the 'child' paves the way for a future change" in the personality.[144] For the individuation process, the symbol of the child anticipates the synthesis of conscious and unconscious elements in the personality and thus is a symbol for uniting the opposites. It is the one that brings healing and the one who makes one feel whole. As a symbol it can have many manifestations. As a sym-

---

143 Jung, Child Archetype,, *Archetypes, CW 9i,* ¶ 273fn.
144 Jung, Child Archetype, *Archetypes, CW 9i,* ¶ 278.

bol for individuation, it must be unifying versus existing only within the collective.

Common to the divine child is its miraculous birth, surviving the adversities of childhood, including abandonment and danger. The child can look like a god or a hero, and although his or her nature is human, he or she is in a semi-divine position. According to Jung,[145] this position represents a synthesis of the divine, not yet humanized, and the human, of the unconscious and conscious aspects. Therefore, the divine child signifies the potential anticipation of approaching wholeness, an individuation process.

The leaders of the three major religions were orphans or had miraculous births. In Christianity, Jesus was a miraculous conception "...for that which is conceived in her is of the Holy Spirit;" according to St. Mark. His was a lowly birth in a manger and yet he was to become the spiritual leader for Christians.

Queen Maya gave birth to the Buddha-to-be, Siddhartha, after being touched by a divine Bodhisattva on a white elephant in a dream who touched her side and she became pregnant. She died seven days after the birth of Siddhartha. Due to a prophecy that his son would either become a great King or a great spiritual leader and teacher, the King insulated him in the palace, and he married, but at age 29 he left the palace after seeing an old man. He then sought to find out the answers to his questions about life and suffering. He learned that neither wealth nor renunciation offered the answers, but rather the Middle Way that was neither self-indulgent nor self-punishing and revolved neither around pleasure or aversion. It was the way that was true to oneself.

In the Muslim faith, Muhammad's father died before he was born and his mother died when he was about five to six years old. He was placed under the care of his paternal grandfather for the next few years until he died and then at about age 8 he was passed to the care of a paternal Uncle. The Qur'an states, "Did God not find you an orphan and give you shelter and care? And He found you wandering, and gave you guid-

---

145 Jung, Child Archetype, *Archetypes, CW 9i*, ¶ 281.

ance. And he found you in need, and made you independent."[146] In his twenties he entered the service of a wealthy family, married the widow who was much older than him and had four daughters. He had visions that were later to become the Qur'an, the holy book of the Muslim faith.

In order to understand the divine child and since the divine child is not human, one must look at what it is trying to tell us symbolically. The divine child has a "miraculous birth," it happens this way to tell us that this is not about a human child; it is about something that is not empirical. "The motifs of 'insignificance,' exposure, abandonment, danger, etc., try to show us how precarious is the psychic possibility of [attaining] wholeness." Jung described this as "the enormous difficulties to be met with in attaining this 'highest good.'"[147] And this is difficult because we often meet environmental obstacles or physical limitations. The divine child can accomplish miraculous deeds, but can also be undone by them. When the divine child archetype has been activated, and especially with the orphan archetype one is in for a hero's journey. Regardless, the hero tries to overcome the obstacle, whatever it might be, and to attain more consciousness, a separation of the dark of unconsciousness and the light of consciousness. In essence, it is overcoming a previous state of unconsciousness.

Sometimes we are inspired by another's encounter with tragedy. For many years, I worked as a pediatric psychologist in a hospital-based setting. I recall working with a 10-year-old boy who while riding his bike was hit by a car and subsequently lost his foot. He was a quiet rather introverted boy who did not say much but fully participated in his rehabilitation. In an effort to assist him with the mourning of this loss, he thought he would like to plant a tree and bury a picture of his lost foot under the roots of this tree. The family pastor was called and a ceremony in the chapel of the hospital was performed in which his life was to be affirmed, and a funeral for the foot could be held. Rather than a casket, a sealed envelop with a photo of the foot was to be buried under the new tree at his home. He was very brave as he verbally spoke at the ceremony and said goodbye to his foot. There was not a dry eye

---

146 Muhammad: Legacy of a Prophet, http://www.pbs.org/muhammad/ timeline_html.shtml, 93:6-8.

147 Jung, Child Archetype, *Archetypes, CW 9i*, ¶ 282.

in the audience! His ability to move through this tragic accident was an inspiration to us all.

The divine child has vitality. He or she is endowed with magical powers and, despite all dangers, survives. There is a deep part within us that has the strength and vigor to deal with life; it is about the urge to be in touch with our own nature and our own powers. Jung thought that this vitality is a law of nature and thus, is an invincible power, even though at the beginning it feels insignificant and improbable. The divine child motif becomes equated with the Self in that one is called to listen and heed the call for potential changes. This then has the potential to lead to differentiation of self from other and as a result, psychic consciousness is possible. This is an agonizing process, but it yields a differentiation that produces insight and consciousness. In essence, the child is a symbol for the Self and its urge toward wholeness.

The Potential

The divine child motif, which as an archetype exists in all of us, and as Jung described, miraculous birth, insignificance, exposure, abandonment, and danger, may also be a vestige memory of one's own childhood, such as forgotten experiences; memories that were there before we had language to put to them, or if there had been trauma that erased those memories. In addition, the child as a symbol could be "'...representing the preconscious childhood aspect of the psyche.'"[148] Regardless, in Jungian psychology the function of the constellation of the archetype at certain times is to compensate one-sidedness or to correct the extravagances of the conscious mind. For this we need the image of the child, the bringer of something new. Specifically, the child motif brings a potential future. A child has a future, which is one of the reasons why it is so difficult when a young child dies. Even in dying, though, the child can teach us about hope.

While working in a Children's Hospital, I occasionally worked with children who were dying and found it difficult, but at the same time a very rewarding experience. I tried to always maintain a hope that this

---

148 Jung, Child Archetype, *Archetypes, CW 9i,* ¶ 273.

particular treatment would bring the necessary remission of the disease, but when I knew it would not, I was embarking on a special journey with a child that would help ease the final transition from life to death. I recall one girl about 7 years old at the time, who was dying from a genetically malformed vital organ. She had no conception of what it would mean to die and no one would talk with her about this. As she increasingly experienced not being able to do what other children could do, I asked her what image she could think of that would be helpful to her when she had to pass from life to death. She thought of an image of an angel who would hold her in her arms. We found a picture of an angel holding a child. This image delighted her, and she often thought of this picture when she experienced stress from procedures in the hospital. Although I could not be there at the time of her death, I was told that it was a very peaceful passing, and I imagined that she was in the arms of the angel. For others who knew of my work there was always the question, "How can you work with a dying child?" For me there was great satisfaction knowing that I might help to facilitate this last transition; this girl taught me about having a soothing inner image for her last transition. Jung has said, "But while the man who despairs marches toward nothingness, the one who has placed his faith in the archetype follows the tracks of life and lives right into his death."[149] The little girl had this wisdom with her image.

This child described above had a miraculous birth and against all odds survived as long as she did. At one point she was able to attend a private school even though she came from a poor family. She survived the adversities of her early childhood and yet had the strength to face her death with a companion. She was facing a hero's journey with strength and fortitude.

"'Child' means something evolving towards independence."[150] The divine child comes into the world with insignificant beginnings and a mysterious and miraculous birth. Jung likened this to the union of the opposites out of which the third comes, neither a yes nor a no, but something new which unites them both. From this comes the numinous

---

149 Jung, *MDR*, p. 284.
150 Jung, Child Archetype, *Archetypes, CW 9i*, ¶ 287.

character of the "child;" it is "a meaningful but unknown content."[151] By virtue of this new beginning, this means that the child must leave the family and detach itself from its origins. For Jung this meant that the child was evolving toward independence, thus, "abandonment is therefore a necessary condition, not just a concomitant symptom."[152] This is symbolized in the myths of the heroes, two of which have already been spoken about.

We also see this in modern day hero stories of Spiderman, Batman, and Harry Potter. As an infant, Lord Voldemort wounded Harry during the murder of his famous wizard parents, James and Lily Potter. A lightning-bolt scar remained on his forehead from the attack. As a symbol, the thunderbolt mythically represents the spark of life and enlightenment that was hurled by Zeus down to earth as a dramatic symbol of god's dual capacity for creation and destruction.[153] The wound whether physical or emotional, was the first evidence of a spiritual calling for this young boy. We also see this with those in the helping professions as the wounded healers. A term coined by Henri Nouwen who describes how our own woundedness can become a source of life for others.[154] It is a calling to do this work, which comes out of the pain of one's experience.

Sometimes in our pain, it is not possible to have a vision for the future. One has to wait for something else to come, a new creation that will yield a new attitude or way. If we cannot do this ourselves we may put it on someone else to do it for us, but this never brings an inner peace. This tendency to attribute to others the drives and complexes that belong to oneself are known as projections, that is, when we ascribe something to someone else that belongs to us, and ultimately the other person will fail us. Then, and usually with disappointment in the other, we must take the projection back and eventually deal with the issue ourselves. What is called for is a higher consciousness, something that enlarges our own awareness to overcome the darkness we might be expe-

151 Jung, Child Archetype, *Archetypes, CW 9i*, ¶ 285.
152 Jung, Child Archetype, *Archetypes, CW 9i*, ¶ 287.
153 G.A. Grynbaum, *The San Francisco Jung Institute Library Journal*, 19 (4), pp. 17-48.
154 H.J.M. Nouwen, *The Wounded Healer*.

riencing. This is very much the individual journey, which can be lonely
at times.

Rebecca was an 11-year-old girl who complained about how unfair
the other girls were to her because they would often not include her
in their play. She felt unwanted, lonely and rejected by her peers. In
her therapy, the feelings of being so alone were validated and once she
felt understood then we could look at what part she played in this. Of
course, this seemed very foreign to her as it was the others who were
being mean to her and that was the problem. But as we looked at her
interactions with her peers it became clear that she was frequently bossy
and pushy and wanted the play to go her way. I role-played the peer
interactions with her and she took the role of the one being bossed.
Now it became apparent to her that what she was accusing others of,
that is, being unfair, she was also doing to them. As she began to see that
this was making her friends withdraw from her, she began to be more
cooperative and less demanding. When she did this, withdrawing the
projection that her peers were mean, then the relationships improved.

Attaining this higher consciousness is like finding oneself now very
different from the affiliated group, which tends not to see things in the
same way. We can go along and think that we are conscious about most
things and then suddenly we can be hit with something that shakes
us. It is like finding oneself apart from the others; suddenly what we
believed no longer holds value.

This is frequently seen in the couple that after many years of marriage
and after the children have left home, no longer find themselves attracted to one another. They have completed their family responsibilities,
but their own personal needs have gone unmet. The collective needs of
belonging to community and raising children have been fulfilled, but
the deeper archetypal needs of being true to oneself eventually become
constellated. The feeling that the other person was not helpful is now
reflected in the disappointment of the other, but these feelings belong
to that of another realm; the realm, perhaps, of their own parent who
could not be there or to ways the person was not true to himself or herself. It becomes so easy to place the blame on the other, when, in fact, it
is about taking responsibility for one's own needs and finding appropri-

ate expression and solutions for these needs. This relates to the feeling of being orphaned because we experience this as feeling all alone with no one there to understand and fulfill the longing. This is also seen in couples that seek a relationship with another person for something that is missing in the current relationship.

Matt had everything. He was handsome, had a beautiful wife, two healthy, bright children, and a good job he liked. However, during his marriage of 15 years he had always had another woman he was seeing for sex. Over the years there were multiple women some lasting a few years and then the relationship would just wither away, but he always encountered another woman without much effort. Everything was going fine with this arrangement until his wife discovered the latest affair. He tried to stop seeing the woman, but could not and when he was discovered a second time, his wife gave him an ultimatum and this is when he entered therapy. At first he was willing to do anything to save the marriage, but when the pressure was off and things improved in the marital relationship, he would call the other woman or have a brief sexual encounter. He did not want to leave his wife for this woman, but saw this relationship as a kind of reward for "being good."

For some months, Matt tried to rationalize his actions, but he had to face himself and his actions and the impact this was having on his marital relationship and his children who were aware things had changed with their parents. This was the hardest thing Matt had to do and he felt very alone in his journey for healing. He had to look at himself and what it meant to be a man, not just a boy who could have whatever he wanted when he wanted it. He also needed support for this from others because this was a life long pattern that needed changing. It was the archetypal energy of the Fool and specifically in this case, Casanova, which gripped him. Historically the fool was a part of the court of the King and Queen to express the joy of life, to entertain them, but also to provide balance to the kingdom by breaking the rules and providing an outlet for forbidden insights, behaviors and feelings. In this case, Matt was acting out forbidden sexual energies by having sex with women with no promise of commitment. However, he had no idea of the pain and suffering he was causing to his family by such behavior. In the therapy, he began to see how he was avoiding intimacy with the one woman he loved the most, his wife. But his journey for healing was one that he had to do alone and face the demons inside him.

Why is the parentless child so important? The symbol of the child without parents indicates a content of the unconscious that is far removed from or very unrelated to the consciousness of the times.[155] It is a part of the psyche that may still be deep within the unconscious, perhaps within the mother archetype, and a problem for which there seems to be no answer. The orphan represents a threat to the social order; it may be trying to right a too one-sided attitude. The orphan is unrelated because he or she does not have parents and new caregivers must be found. Is it that the child must live a destiny that necessitates an individual journey, an individuation? It seems important to take a look at what the orphan potential holds for us and in each of us. What is missing?

In fairy tales often the old king is in need of renewal as he symbolizes worn-out doctrines or expressions of archetypes that have lost their originality and emotional impact,[156] or there is the childless couple that cannot conceive. The king has no partner or the couple is sterile. In psychological terms there is no emotion, no feeling, or irrational element that can consciously be related to, that is, no renewal can develop. For the childless couple, the opposites, spirit and nature, masculine and feminine, consciousness and unconsciousness, become dissociated. If something new is to come, their needs to be experienced an unrest, a suffering of the tension of opposites so that something can be born. The symbolic child comes because an old attitude has had to die.

It is from myths and fairy tales that one meets the notion of the divine child, and it is in these settings that the child plays a central role. This is taken up more in the analysis of the fairy tale of The Little Orphan Girl in Chapter 5. In any case, the birth of the orphan child happens under peculiar circumstances: often it is a childless couple, a divine birth, an abandoned child, saved by other humans or animals, and this child grows up to be a hero or a god. Jung stated that the divine child "is a wonder-child, begotten, born, and brought up in quite extraordinary circumstances, and not—this is the point—a human child."[157] This

---

155 J. Hill, *The Tristan Legend: A Confrontation Between Logos and Eros.*
156 Hill, *The Tristan Legend.*
157 Jung, Child Archetype, *Archetypes, CW 9i,* ¶ 273fn.

child, thus, has a link with the past because it is of an archetypal nature, "a psychic organ present in all of us."[158] We are touched by the divine child, because it exists in all of us.

The Isolation

The archetype, which represents an inner psychic fact, has two poles, one that is positive and one that is negative or one that is conscious and one that is unconscious, or one that could be pointing backwards and one pointing forwards. And there are masculine and feminine components. The symbol becomes dead when it no longer holds any meaning and when "the nourishing source of the image no longer reaches it."[159] When this happens we lack energy and relationships, for example, we become flat and not very interesting. In addition, the divine child with all its potential also has a negative side and in the case of the orphan there is the potential to remain isolated and mistrustful of the world. This tendency to remain isolated and mistrustful is, of course, understandable given the very difficult beginnings, but this can only maintain the suffering.

Melanie was 57 years old when her husband of 22 years died suddenly. She was taken by surprise and continued to work for the next three years until plagued by back problems, which forced her to retire early from her job as an accountant. She went to live with her brother who was five years older and newly retired from his job. She thought this would be a good idea since she could be there to take care of him and she could live less expensively. However, this required she move to a new city some distance from their home and the few friends she had. As a result she became increasingly isolated and did little outside the home in the way of social activities for herself. Six years later her brother died and she found herself wondering what was the meaning of life. She questioned why she would still be alive. She had lived to serve others, and now there was no one to serve. She had to face herself and her history and her meaning. Melanie became interested in her ancestors and researched members of the family putting together a story about her

---

158 Jung, Child Archetype, *Archetypes, CW 9i*, ¶ 271.
159 J. Jacobi, *Complex/Archetype/Symbol*, p. 96.

family, which she hoped to leave to her grown children. For her going back to her roots was a beginning to connect to her ancestors and to review her life. Now finally alone she has the time and energy to look at the meaning of her life.

This does not mean that one has to be literally alone to do this work, but it does mean that one has to carve out space and time for the journey to discover the meaning of one's life. Frequently we become so busy managing life that there is little time for such endeavors, but this space is crucial especially as we age because we run out of time and resources and the psyche is always trying to lead us toward wholeness as long as we are on this earth.

At this point it may be useful to discuss what is a symbol. Every symbol has an archetypal core, but not every archetype is a symbol, the archetype exists only in potential to become a symbol. The conversion into a symbol happens when the raw material provided by the collective unconscious enters into relation with the conscious mind and its form-giving character, the archetype, become representable as a concrete image, an archetypal image, a symbol. The archetype can be thought of as psychic energy with the symbol providing the manifestation by which the archetype becomes known. This potential exists in everyone and exists *a priori*.

Thus, the representation of the child motif can take on diverse symbolic meanings. For example, when the child appears in dreams it could be things from one's childhood that are forgotten, or it could be compensating for or correcting an often one-sided nature of adult consciousness, or it could possibly be a direct symbol of future possibilities. When the symbol appears as a divine or heroic child, according to Jung, it is primarily a symbol of the self. And as previously mentioned it could be an encounter with the dark side of God. There are always two sides, two poles to every symbol.

The experience of isolation can occur at very young ages. Mario Jacoby reviews the psychology of the infant in his book, *Jungian Psychotherapy and Contemporary Infant Research*, and shows through the various theories how the relationship with the primary caregiver, usually the mother, is so important. According to Jung, the unconscious background of the parents influences the child because "children are so deeply involved in the psychological attitude of their parents that it is no wonder that most of the nervous disturbances in childhood can be traced back to a disturbed psychic atmosphere in the home."[160] He even goes so far to say, "Parents should always be conscious of the fact that they themselves are the principal cause of neurosis in their children."[161]

In contemporary child work, the "infant is now known to play a far greater part in the mother-infant relationship than was previously thought possible. Indeed, an infant is born with a characteristic personality that is highly individual, and furthermore, his perceptual capacities are quite well advanced."[162] Thus, it is a bi-directional relationship and one in which the histories of both parties, the parent and the child, need to be explored. A normal amount of frustration must occur in the relationship in order for it to become real, that is, that one can have both good and bad feelings about another. In reality, we must all leave paradise and face life for all its offerings and tragedies.

The orphan journey as previously described by Jung and in myth and fairy tale is one who is on a solitary journey. Jung even commented that to be on the "in-dividual" journey one is all alone in the world.[163] The image of the orphan is also a symbol that each of us must confront our own individuality and that can only be done alone in relationship to one's self. Could this feeling of being so alone in the world be a reminder of something that each of us has to face? We are certainly not alone in the world with these feelings; many people feel this way.

---

160   Jung, Structure, *Structure and Dynamics, CW 8,* ¶ 80.
161   Jung, Structure, *Structure and Dynamics, CW 8,* ¶ 84.
162   Fordham in Sidoli & Davies, *Jungian Child Psychotherapy: Individuation in Childhood,* p. 40.
163   Jung, The Relations Between the Ego and the Unconscious. *Two Essays on Analytical Psychology, CW 7,* ¶ 266.

The Survival

In myth, the child god is usually an abandoned foundling[164] and, as has been previously mentioned, it is threatened by extraordinary dangers. However, the child survives despite all the overwhelming circumstances and threats. The orphan is a survivor. Recall the story of the American orphan who survived a difficult childhood to hold a respectable job in Chapter 2.

Kerenyi[165] talked about the child god seeming to possess a biographical significance that we have denied ourselves as humans. We seem to have lost the feeling that we all possess a divine nature. The image of the child transports one into a place that is wondrous and fantastic. Being in this place evokes the god's ability to do extraordinary feats even though he or she is a child.

Overcoming dangers are seen in Zeus's surviving being devoured and of Dionysus surviving being torn to pieces by the Titans. The mother often has an interesting part in the story. She can abandon the child; she can die at the time of the child's birth, or be violently separated from her child. There are various versions of the birth of Zeus, but one tells of Rhea, his mother, giving Kronos a wrapped up stone as a substitute for the son. Recall Kronos, destined to be overthrown by a powerful son, devoured all his sons and hence sought to do away with all male children.[166] In one story, Hera, his sister, takes Zeus to Crete and he is hung on the branch of a tree so that he will not be discovered in heaven, earth, or sea, thus his mother abandons the child god. In another tale, Zeus is hidden in a cave and is fed by the bees. Regardless, the main theme is that Zeus was born, was abandoned[167] by his mother, and left to the elements in which he had to survive. In one variation, the wild beasts nurse Zeus, which illustrates the fact that the orphan is solitary, and that he is at home in the primeval world.

---

164 C. Kerenyi, *Essays on a Science of Mythology: The Myth of the Divine Child and the Mysteries of Eleusis.*

165 Kerenyi, *Essays.*

166 Kerenyi, *The Gods of the Greeks.*

167 Kerenyi, *Essays.*

Jung has questioned why the birth of the hero, often the orphan, takes place under extraordinary circumstances.[168] Jung states, "… the hero is not born like an ordinary mortal because his birth is a rebirth from the mother-wife." In this dual-mother motif, one of the mothers is the real human mother, and the other is the symbolic mother with the first birth making him the real man and the second an immortal half-god. This symbol, thus, suggests the extraordinary birth and the potential for the journey to finding meaning beyond the ordinary. The foster-mother can be an animal as previously seen in the she-wolf of Romulus and Remus. We also see this in baptism within Christianity where one is born again in a mysterious manner and thus partakes of divinity.[169]

The orphan child is often in mythology and fairy tale left all on its own after the death of its father and mother, and there are stories of terrible beatings and sufferings. However, according to Kerenyi, "From the miserable plight of the orphan there emerges a god."[170] It is the turning of this misfortune that is impressive and significant. It is the survival and now turning this into something that can be more productive and worthwhile for the orphan. However, it would be naive to think that all such people are looking for or wanting or can have an epiphany, a manifestation of the god within. That is what von Franz[171] talked about as being open to the unknown stranger. Sometimes the epiphany just happens.

I recall a man who was hospitalized with his first heart attack at age 83. While he was in intensive care his church minister brought him the Sunday Bulletin, which had the poem "Cana" by Thomas Merton written in 1946.

---

168   Jung, The Dual Mother, *Symbols of Transformation*, CW 5, ¶ 493.
169   Jung, Dual Mother, *Symbols*, CW 5, ¶ 494.
170   Kerenyi, *Essays*, p. 32.
171   von Franz, *Archetypal Dimensions of the Psyche*.

Cana

Once when our eyes were clean as noon, our rooms
Filled with the joys of Cana's feast:
For Jesus came, and His disciples, and His Mother,
And after them the singers
And some men with violins.

Once when our minds were Galilees,
And clean as skies our faces,
Our simple rooms were charmed with sun.

Our thoughts went in and out in whiter coats than
God's disciples,
In Cana's crowded rooms, at Cana's tables.

Nor did we seem to fear the wine would fail:
For ready, in a row, to fill with water and a miracle,
We saw our earthen vessels, waiting empty.
What wine those humble waterjars foretell!

Wine for the ones who, bended to the dirty earth,
Have feared, since lovely Eden, the sun's fire,
Yet hardly mumble, in their dusty mouths, one prayer.

Wine for old Adam, digging in the briars!
Merton[172]

The poem went unread until 2 weeks later when he was on the car-
diac unit recovering from open-heart surgery. He was feeling depressed,
was recovering from the surgery, had developed pneumonia, and had
symptoms of kidney failure. Suddenly, he thought about the poem and
read it to himself. Then a young woman nurse came in and was sur-

---

172 T. Merton, *The Collected Poems of Thomas Merton*, p. 93.

prised to see him sitting up as he had been just curled up in bed facing the wall since his arrival there, not caring whether he lived or died. He asked to read the poem to her and as he did he watched her reactions and she said once he finished, "In all my years of Sunday school I never heard such a profound reading of that story." At that point he became overwhelmed by emotion and began sobbing uncontrollably.

The Bible story is about the first miracle when Jesus turned the water into wine at the wedding feast. For this man, there came an epiphany from not only reading the poem, but also having a validating witness. For the first time he became in touch with himself. He later told me that he grew up in a home in which he always felt alone. He had a sister who was 8 years older and 2 parents who from his perspective had little interest in him as a person. He said he created what he called "weather stations" in the house, which would let him know what kind of mood his mother was in, and then he would know how to behave according to these moods. In order to relate, he had to know what the emotional status of the other was, not what was in his true nature. With this experience, he went into a therapy, which allowed him to face his true inner feelings.

The nurse who was present was like the unknown visitor that von Franz[173] discussed in her book, *Archetypal Dimensions of the Psyche*. The unknown visitor came from nowhere and if one opens the door then the individuation process can begin. Of course, the opening up of dialogue to this unknown visitor, this coming of the gods, depends on our attitude toward him or her. This attitude then determines whether the visitor becomes a blessing or a disaster.

This is illustrated by the story of Baucis and Philemon as told in *Bulfinch's Mythology*. The story is told about the time when Jupiter and his son Mercury came to visit Phrygia a country with good habitable land. They presented themselves as weary travelers and were turned away by many on whose doors they knocked. Then they came to the humble home of Baucis and her husband Philemon who had been married a long time. They were not ashamed of their poverty and made their life endurable by moderate desires and kindly deeds. They welcomed the

---

173   von Franz, *Archetypal Dimensions*.

strangers, cleared a space for them at the table, in which one leg was shorter than the others, and kindled up a fire, began to prepare a meal and gave them water in which to clean themselves. The setting was simple, but they rubbed the table with sweet smelling herbs, and made a stew from what they had. All the while they engaged in lively conversation bestowing friendly faces and a hearty welcome.

The couple noticed that as soon as the wine was poured out, it renewed itself in the pitcher of its own accord. Baucis and Philemon were struck with terror when they then recognized their heavenly guests and fell to their knees and begged forgiveness for their poor entertainment. They then offered to kill an old goose which they kept as a guardian to their humble abode and asked the gods to take this as a sacrifice in honor of their guests. The goose was nimble and difficult to catch and when the gods saw their intentions they forbade it to be slain.

The couple was then taken to the top of a mountain and told that those who had been inhospitable would pay a penalty, but that they would go free from any chastisement. Bacuis and Philemon then witnessed all the country was sunk into a lake except for their home. They then saw their house to be changed into a temple with a gilded roof and marble floors, carved doors and ornaments of gold. Jupiter then asked them to tell him their wishes, and after conferring they said, "We ask to be priests and guardians of this your temple; and since here we have passed our lives in love and concord, we wish that one and the same hour may take us both from life, that I may not live to see her grave, nor be laid in my own by her."[174] Their wish was granted and when they reached the end of their lives, they were changed into two trees standing side by side.

Here we have a personal encounter with the divine. At the time this tale was told there was a patriarchal order where power prevailed over interpersonal Eros, and thus, the story was a compensation for needed relationship. As von Franz tells, "meeting the gods is always a surprise" because "they appear as unknown, inconspicuous, disguised visitors." And these meetings tend to come *when personal encounter with and individual relationship to the divine has become a necessity*, outside the

---

174 *Bulfinch's Mythology*, p. 46.

institutionalized forms and views of religious life."[175] The encounters we have with others have the potential to bring meaning, but we must be open and willing to open the door to such encounters.

The birth of the orphan is fraught with adversity and in myth and fairy tale the real life of the human child is also mirrored. That is, the infant who grows up either truly orphaned or with the feeling of being orphaned has a very early history of having to be on his or her own at a time when he or she is most vulnerable or as previously discussed of feeling alone and unseen.

The surviving is not at question, because within our human nature we do have ways of adapting; in fact, the adaptation has helped the orphan to survive. Nevertheless, the surviving does not help one to be in touch with his true nature, which has been lost. It is a fate in which the child is exposed to all the elements and experiences persecution, but the fate is also the triumph of the orphan. It is the symbolic orphanhood, which gives it the significance because it expresses the primal solitude.

The preceding has attempted to relate the mythology to the human and to do this is quite reductionistic when, in fact, we are really trying to stay within the world of the symbolic. "The world tells us what *is* in the world and what is *true* in the world," but "a 'symbol' is . . . an image presented by the world itself."[176] The fate of the orphan child gods evolved from cosmic life, and it is a fate that transcends the individual phenomenon.

In order to understand what that fate might look like, it will be interesting to look specifically at a fairy tale. In the following tale we are able to see how the symbol of the orphan relates to the individual psyche.

---

175 von Franz, *Archetypal Dimensions*, p. 59.
176 Kerenyi, *Essays*, p. 45.

Chapter 5

FAIRY TALE: THE LITTLE ORPHAN GIRL

> In myths and fairytales, as in dreams, the psyche tells its own
> story, and the interplay of the archetypes is revealed in its
> natural setting as "formation, transformation / the eternal
> Mind's eternal recreation."
>
> C.G. Jung[177]

The fairy tale gives us an opportunity to look further at the symbolism
of the orphan. A fairy tale allows us to point out parallels to psychic processes that occur in everyday life. Moreover in Jungian psychology, the
fairy tale is an expression of the collective unconscious, and thus, presents typical responses to typical human problems. These responses and
expressions come from the creative aspect of the unconscious and hence
are appropriate to our discussion of the orphan. The fairy tale is interpreted subjectively, as symbols of the many facets of a single personality.

This is a fairy tale from Chile. The early history of Chile is largely
about a race struggle between the Spaniards and the Araucanians, the
native people, whom the Spaniards first encountered in 1541.[178] After
hundreds of years of struggle these two groups finally reached a peaceful

---

177 Jung, The Phenomenology of the Spirit in Fairytales, *The Archetypes and
the Collective Unconscious, CW 9i,* ¶ 400.
178 Y. Pino-Saavedra, *Folktales of Chile.*

settlement in 1884. Geographically, Chile is located between the Andes Mountains and the Pacific Ocean on the west coast of South America and falls into four regions that correspond to four folk traditions. This tale most likely has its origins in the southern part of Chile. In the south the setting is the forest, and the men who gather coal are the principal characters of the folklore, as is the father in this tale.

The native Araucanian people fall somewhere between the high Inca and Aztec civilizations and the lower nomadic tribes of hunters and food gatherers. The race was considered to have heroic leaders who fought the Spaniards, and today they have maintained a cultural identity, although Chile has a large European community. As a result, these people have a narrative tradition of folklore, which is known for contact with the supernatural. This folklore tradition functions "to entertain people during long funerals, at community work such as shelling corn, at social gatherings, or even to assist suitors in fixing the minds of their sweethearts on amorous adventures."[179] Regardless, there is a rich Catholic influence, although this has not caused the tales to lose their original essence.[180]

This tale is known as Tale-Type 432: the Prince as bird. The tale of the bird lover appears several times in medieval literature, notably in Marie de-France's *Yonec*. This type of story was most likely current in Italy during the Renaissance and is popular in the Mediterranean countries today. Madame d'Aulnoy published the tale in France in 1702 and from this version the tale became popular in Scandinavia.[181] According to Thompson, there are gaps in places the tale was told—the tale has not been collected in Germany or the rest of northwest Europe, the British Isles, or the western Slavic countries. However, there are versions in Russia, India, and Africa. There are also versions in North America from Canada to New Mexico and in South America. It is considered an ordinary folktale of a supernatural nature.

The motif is as follows:

---

179 Pino-Saavedra, *Folktales of Chile*, p. xxxv.
180 Pino-Saavedra, *Folktales of Chile*.
181 S. Thompson, *The Folktale*.

1. The Bird Lover. A prince in the form of a bird flies to a beautiful maiden; when in her presence he becomes a man.

2. The Lover Wounded. The cruel stepmother (sister) severely wounds him with a knife, a thorn, or a glass placed on the window-ledge.

3. The Lover Healed. The maiden follows her lover and on the way overhears a conversation of animals or witches how he may be healed. She follows their directions and heals him.[182]

Other fairy tales with this motif include "The Greenish Bird,"[183] "The Earl of Mar's Daughter,"[184] and "King Bean."[185] Thus, the tale follows a common pattern, and from this pattern the tale is discussed. First the entire tale is told.

The Tale

The Little Orphan Girl

There was once a married couple who worked faithfully their whole lives as coal gatherers for a very wealthy rancher who lived in the mountains. This couple had a single daughter and a dog. The wife died one day, and with the years, the husband followed her, charging his daughter to bury him behind the ranch beside his wife's body. He warned her not to tell anyone that she was alone so that people would continue to respect her.

After a year had passed, and finally the nearest neighbors, who were a mother and two daughters, realized that the girl was all alone. Meanwhile, a voice surprised her in the house one afternoon. "Leave a washbowl of water just inside your door, for I wish to keep you company." She looked all about and saw only a little bird perched on the branch of a tree in the dooryard. She agreed gladly and left a bowl of water. That

---

182 A. Aarne, *The Types of Folktale*, pp. 146-147.

183 A. Paredes, *Folktales of Mexico*.

184 K. Briggs, *A Dictionary of British Folk-Tales in the English Language, Part A, (Vol. 1)*.

185 S. Thompson, *One Hundred Favorite Folktales*.

evening when she lay down to sleep, the girl heard a little bird bathing himself in the bowl, and at the very same moment a young man sat down on the bed to talk to her. He offered to visit her the following night as well, and immediately disappeared. At the same hour the next evening, she placed the bowl of water by her door and went to bed to wait. The youth came again, and soon they were intimate friends. He filled her life with all she had lacked.

Meanwhile, the neighbor women were discussing the idea of offering the girl some company and seeing, incidentally, what she did all by herself in that lonely little cottage. They had nicknamed her "*La Guacha*" [Little Orphan]. One afternoon the older daughter from next door strolled over to pay a visit. Although the little orphan refused to let her stay, her efforts were in vain, for her neighbor simply climbed into bed for the night. The girl didn't place the bowl by the door. Later she felt the desperation of the bird as it fluttered down into the room. The lodger slept very well, and in the morning went home to report to her mother, "*La Guacha* sleeps alone."

"The trouble is that you surely fell asleep," answered the old lady.

"Well, of course, I couldn't help it," protested her daughter.

"Then tonight your sister will go. Let's see how she makes out."

It was just like the first time. The younger sister forced herself upon the poor orphan and stayed the night. The girl didn't place the water this time either. When the sister returned home the following day, she declared, "*La Guacha* sleeps alone." But her mother, not at all satisfied, ordered her not to shut her eyes the next time.

The second time, the visitor changed the hour of her arrival. Since the girl had not set the water out for two nights in a row, she had left the bowl this time in hopes of seeing her friend and telling him what was happening. Now, before the neighboring sister left the orphan's house, her mother gave her three razor-sharp knives and said, "If you see water in the room, you must get up and say that you need to go outside. Then put the knives on the bowl with the water."

The orphan and her unwelcome guest went to sleep as usual that evening. About the time dawn was breaking, the neighbor girl heard the bird fluttering with great difficulty. She got up and saw that the room and the bowl itself were covered with blood. With that, she picked up her knives and went home to tell her mother what had happened.

When the little orphan awoke some time after, she saw the same horrible sight. Everything was smeared with blood. She vowed then and there to wander over the whole world until she found him whom she had lost. Leaving her dog alone and putting on her father's clothes, she disguised herself as a hermit and set off on the lonely road. For a weapon, she carried an ancient sword which had belonged to her father. Night came upon her as she was descending the hills, so she searched out some *patagua* [a name of Araucanian origin for *Crimodrendon patagua*, a tree bearing white flowers] shrubs and climbed into one for refuge. Nearby was a pond with some ashes on the bank.

"God only knows who's camping there," she thought, fearing that there must be some bad men about. Great was her surprise when at midnight three ducks arrived and began to wallow in the ashes. The orphan recognized them as the three neighbor women. They had kindled a fire and sat down to talk.

"What do you suppose *La Guacha* will say now that her little bird must be dead?" piped up the younger daughter.

"Today I was in the palace," answered the mother, "and the queen has issued a proclamation, that she will permit anyone to enter the palace who can bring the sick prince a remedy. But nobody will succeed in this."

"Mama," spoke up the older daughter, "you must know what is needed to heal the prince and cure those wounds of his."

"You've got your nose out for news," retorted her mother. "But I'm going to tell you, even though I ought not to. The prince can rise hale and hearty only if he is cured by a feather dipped in our blood. And when, pray tell, is he going to get that?"

"Let's be off to sleep," chorused the three ducks. "Day is about to break now." And letting themselves slide into the water, they swam quacking away.

Immediately the orphan girl climbed out of her bush and ran, with her heart full of vengeance, all the way to her house. A new day had already begun when she went to her room and took a very thick earthenware bottle. Then she headed straight for the house of the three neighboring witches, who always slept in one bed. She sliced off the three sleeping heads with her sword and took their blood until the bottle was filled. Following her footsteps toward home, she sat down about three in the afternoon to rest on a little log. Out of nowhere an old man approached her and asked, "Where are you going, my child?"

"My father is sick, and I'm in search of some remedy."

"He could never be sicker than the prince," answered the old man. "You should see how the king and queen are carrying on and mourning. The palace is all dark with their sadness. The prince lay dying this very morning, and there is free passage for whoever wishes to give him a remedy."

Upon hearing that, she jumped up sharply and set off at a run. From everyone she met on the road, she inquired breathlessly, "Is it true that the prince is gravely ill?" She always received the same reply, "Terribly grave. He won't live through the day." She met a boy on the road and asked him for the location of the palace.

"Do you have some medicine for him?" he asked.

"Yes, yes," she gasped, exhausted from her race.

"Then let's run faster," he replied. "You might be able to arrive while the prince is still alive."

When the girl got to the palace gate at last, everyone who saw her disguised in her father's clothes let out a shout of gladness. "There's an old man at the door who has come with a remedy for the prince." They notified the queen, who said mournfully, "It seems like a lost cause, for now he can hardly breathe. But since this is the last person and he is so old, let him come in."

Coming to the prince's bedside, the girl said in a gruff, manly voice, "Everyone go out of the room. Leave me alone with the prince." When they had all obeyed in order to see his prodigy, she took the bottle out of her jacket and dipped a feather in the blood. She began to cure the prince's wounds, especially a gaping one at his throat which practically separated his head from his trunk. As soon as the remedy was applied, his flesh drew together. The miracle was done, and the prince was healed. He sat up in bed, and looking straight at the old fellow, said, "You have saved me old man. I shall give you whatever you ask."

"That's not important," said she. "I only ask for the ring you have on your hand as a remembrance."

Then the prince rang a bell beside the bed. The queen and all the court came running, for the bell was rung only when the prince needed to be together with everybody. Thronged in the doorway, they found him dressed and healed of his wounds. Just at this moment, the little old man slipped unobtrusively away through the crowd. The only one to see him was the queen, who said, "You must never leave my side, for I believe that you have healed my son."

"You may pay me, madam, with that ring you are wearing on your right hand." This ring carried a portrait of the prince. The queen immediately took it off and passed it to the old man. Then she dashed off in great excitement to see her son. The queen thought that the old hermit would wait for her, but the disguised orphan girl slipped away and returned to her own cottage.

Several days passed, and she fulfilled her vow by placing the bowl of water night after night. The bird didn't come. Finally she said sadly, "He's angry with me, and the whole thing is unfair." It was great and joyous surprise for her when she heard the fluttering of wings one night. She was sleeping with her hands resting on her breast and the two rings placed on her fingers. But this time the young man had come with his sword unsheathed and with the intention of killing her in vengeance for the knives. Hearing the noise, she started up in bed and the sparkle of jewels caught the prince's eye. He recognized his own ring and remembered the gift he had presented to the old man. Immediately he fell to his knees to beg her pardon, and she told him the whole story of the witches, whose corpses were still to be found in bed at the neighboring house.

When her innocence was proved, the prince took her up and carried her to the palace to be his wife with the king and queen's consent. The newlyweds received the crowns of the kingdom, while the old royal couple stayed on as guests at the palace. The little orphan and her prince lived happily for many years after this.[186]

The Interpretation

The tale is discussed from each of the motif headings previously mentioned. In each area the orphan as symbolically represented in an individuation process is discussed and then summarized at the end.

The Bird Lover

The story begins with a married couple that worked faithfully as coal gatherers for a wealthy rancher who lived in the mountains. They have an only daughter and a dog. Then the mother dies and then the father dies and she becomes an orphan, that is, she is now without parents. This state of being alone is not a favorable state in the tale, and she hears a voice that tells her to leave a washbowl of water just inside her door, which she does gladly. Then she is visited nightly by a bird that transforms into a young man who becomes her companion and fills "her life with all she had lacked."

Thus, in the beginning we have a girl who is all alone, without a mother, who has died, and then without a father, who tells her to bury

---

186 Pino-Saavedra, *Folktales of Chile*. pp. 81-85.

him next to his wife behind the ranch. The father warns her not to tell anyone of her circumstances of being all alone.

In terms of her feminine development there are three levels that become apparent. On the first level there is the idea that one is living in a patriarchal state and the feminine is not valued enough and so it turns negative; the task is to give back value to the feminine. The second level is the individual case of the orphan, which is the personal negative mother complex, as described below, and the task is to come in relationship with the feminine. The third level is the individuation process, which will be discussed later.

Subjectively, the tale is of a girl who has first of all lost her mother, and thus due to insufficient mothering, will have a negative mother complex. This is like the child, whose mother has not been there enough emotionally to provide adequate mirroring and validation for the child and, in the case of a girl, has not been around long enough for her to learn the feminine way.

Of course, in the tale we do not know how old this girl was when the mother died, but from the perspective from which we have been looking at the feeling of being orphaned, we can surmise it was at a young age, and there were no positive female substitutes for her. Without adequate mothering there is no way to learn about feelings, patience, and a sense of being in relationship. When a mother is lacking one loses trust or becomes naive in relationships.

However, she has a father for a while, and she has had him for a longer time than her mother. From our fathers we learn how to be out in the world because the masculine is directed toward the outer world and with taking a stance, but he cautions her to not let anyone know she is alone. Thus, there is a protective attitude he conveys, and one suspects she is a father's daughter and she is living a one-sided life, alone without others. In reality the father gives the child an inner structure; it is an ego development that says you are not helpless and can do things for yourself. In general, this is what parents do for children. The mother gives the feeling tone and a sense of being in relationship. If one has a good-enough father then one would have internalized tradition, consciousness, morality, aggression, and an ability to structure the outer life; it is an ability to say yes or no. These qualities of an internal father image will later turn into an animus figure, her inner image of a man. However, on the collective level there is the patriarchal culture, which keeps her serving the masculine and not the feminine.

How does this feeling of being an orphan become constellated? In this tale, as previously mentioned, the mother complex is negative because the child had so little time with her mother. The mother not being there, missing, is more negative because she is the first caretaker and the father is secondary in the early development. There is not enough strength from the feminine identity, and this is where she needs to grow. In the tale she has a strong bonding to the father because she obeys him and stays close to him, and thus, the task is to develop the feminine. She has to develop her own identity, authenticity, and leave the father.

In terms of the orphan, a single person, the number one is important because it claims an exceptional position. According to Jung,[187] "one is not a number at all; the first number is two. Two is the first number because, with it, separation and multiplication begin, which alone make counting possible." Thus, the second and the third are important for a person's own development, because according to Jung, "ultimately individuation has two principal aspects: in the first place it is an internal and subjective process of integration, and in the second it is an equally indispensable process of objective relationship."[188] This becomes clearer when we talk about the symbolism of the number three.

All seems to go well, she continues to live in her parents' house, and then she hears a voice that tells her to leave a washbowl of water out and when she does a bird transforms into a man to keep her company. In Jungian psychology, the voice might represent a message from the unconscious that a development in ego functioning needs to happen. "It is the impulse from the unconscious that causes the neurotic disturbance in its attempts to get the child onto a higher level of consciousness, to build up a stronger ego complex."[189]

---

187 Jung, Dogma of the Trinity *Psychology and Religion, CW 11*, ¶ 180.
188 Jung, The Psychology of the Transference, *The Practice of Psychotherapy, CW 16*, ¶ 448.
189 von Franz, *The Feminine in Fairy Tales*, p. 20.

This opportunity comes from the inner male (animus) voice, that facilitates her relationship with the unconscious, but this often propels us into adventures so that growth, as painful as it might be, can occur. The bowl of water suggests a container for this process to occur in which she can become closer in touch with the water of life, and to her genuine self.

However, this occurs at night, and thus, is still within the unconscious realm. In order to gain consciousness, something more has to happen, and it is then that the neighbors visit. These women represent the negative feminine and are intrusive in her life, but she does not trust her feelings and so allows them into her house, not realizing what will happen. Nevertheless, these unwelcome visitors are needed to facilitate her growth.

These women portray shadow aspects, perhaps, a lack of trust in the feminine. The negative mother in this instance says all men are bad, and there is a jealousy going on amongst the women. Jealousy and envy come up in the negative mother complex. For example, in this tale there is disbelief that anyone can be happy being alone. The neighbors cannot seem to let the girl live in peace by herself; they are curious and intrusive in her life. This goes on in the personal complex as well as in the collective. In a patriarchal culture women can be jealous of men and the power that men have; they at least want to have the same power as men. Every time the feminine is not allowed to be in relationship then there is envy and criticalness and Eros is killed. That is, it is not possible to have a relationship by fighting with people all the time; there needs to be an element of trust and relatedness.

In this tale, there is a lack of trust in Eros and relationship. The bird in this tale is a positive spirit emerging; it is an intuition of spirit that is coming, and the little orphan girl cannot stay as the daughter of the father because she needs to grow up. In addition, there is the negative mother as exemplified by the neighbor who is suspicious and ill spirited in trying to find out what is going on with the little orphan girl. She acts with conviction, coldness and lack of relatedness exemplifying a negative animus. One can have an animus that is related to the father, an animus with strong values, but this is not one's very own spirit. The little orphan girl has to develop her own spirit, her own sense of being, which is not her father's. However, going forward with one's life is not so easy to do especially when one is very close and beholding to the father who was there after the mother's death. At some point our parents die, and there is a time for mourning the loss. When this time comes it also presents an opportunity for growth.

I knew a middle-aged woman who lost her mother at age 10. When this happened her father announced to her, "Now we will always be here for each other." While this was comforting on one hand, it also served to cut off her life because she remained faithful to that pact until her father died. In fact she had at one point fallen in love with a man, and the father did not approve criticizing his European ancestry. She could not go against her father's wishes. It was only after his death, her experience of the orphan archetype and resultant suffering, that she sought to face who she was and what she could do with her life.

In order to separate from the father, one has to develop one's own personal being and not rely solely on the father's attitude. A positive father can turn negative if the girl is too rigid in herself, for example, sticking too rigidly to rules. Thus, it is important to change and transform values that are not working for her and to develop her own spirituality. One learns from the father image how to defend oneself in this world and then open oneself to new structures and new relationships. All this has to be established and then opened up to her individual way, and this is no easy task as we see in this tale.

The Wounded Lover

The orphan must learn to be more critical in her thinking and have faith. This is a story with a positive father and negative mother complex so she has to heal her animus and rid herself of the negative mother complex. Only the blood of these witches can heal the animus; it is calling for a sacrifice. In some ways she is challenged to transform, but there is doubt. This is often the case when we are challenged with something new and have to find a new way of doing things. The old ways do not work, but we do not know if the new ways will either. Sometimes the unconscious is ambivalent; it wants her to be transformed, but it also wants her to remain unconscious. That is, the self strives toward wholeness, but is very dependent upon the attitude of the ego; if the ego is not willing to cooperate then there is no individuation. This can be seen in those individuals who have suffered early wounding and for whom there is insufficient ego strength to undergo this kind of journey.

The neighbor's daughters force themselves upon the orphan, and she cannot say no and hence a part of her goes unattended. The bird flutters without any connections to the water of life. However, in the third visit, the little orphan girl becomes increasingly challenged to transform. Thus, the daughter of the witch leaves the three razor sharp knives in the bowl of water. The bird becomes wounded, leaving the room and the bowl covered with blood.

The number three is important in this tale; there are three witches, three knives, and she rests at three o'clock. Three is a number with special characteristics because the "One" and the "Other" form an opposition out of which the third comes. Jung[190] described it this way, "But every tension of opposites culminates in a release, out of which comes the 'third.' In the third, the tension is resolved and the lost unity is restored. Three therefore appears as a suitable synonym for a process of development in time." Therefore, "out of one comes two, but from the pairing of these two comes the third."[191] Three, thus, introduces a directional element and serves as a symbol of a dynamic process.[192] According to Jung,[193] the triadic form represents the flow of psychic energy indicating a connection with time and fate. At this point in the tale there seems to be something that wants to become conscious.

In an individual psyche, the bridge between the ego and the self is cut off, and the animus has been wounded. Up until this point, the girl had been very happy with her night bird lover, but it was really not going anywhere, and this rather paradoxical union needs to be challenged to grow up. As an orphan, she is called to go further.

---

190   Jung, Dogma of the Trinity *Psychology and Religion, CW 11*, ¶ 180.
191   von Franz, *Number and Time: Reflections Leading Toward Unification of Depth Psychology and Physics*, p. 103.
192   von Franz, *Number and Time.*
193   Jung, *Children's Dreams.*

So the feminine must go into the depths of her unconscious to discover how this can be transformed. She vows to wander the whole world until she has found him who she lost. This shows the intensity with which this challenge must be faced.

The unconscious holds much energy, and every step to consciousness is a fight along the way. The ego is in the middle and is the center of consciousness, but not consciousness itself. The unconscious is the primary state of being; we are born unconscious and then the ego develops. Even though we are mostly unconscious, the unconscious is a source of energy for our life; thus, every step toward consciousness is to tear some of that energy out of the unconscious. If we think of the unconscious as the natural state then it is clear why we have to fight for consciousness. Sometimes the unconscious helps us to become more aware of what is needed in one's life, but being unconscious means to be alone without an ego to acknowledge the power. Thus, paying attention to these messages from the unconscious is very important because integration is possible.

The ego and the self must be in dialogue with each other in order for there to be increased awareness. There is an evaluation in consciousness, an interest from the soul to be more conscious. Hence, if one does not continue to work on this, the creative energy that allows one to optimize individual potential is lost.

The Lover Healed

In the tale, the orphan leaves her home and is disguised as a hermit wearing her father's clothes, and she sets off on "the lonely road." The journey is a lonely one because she can only go it alone. She carries her father's sword, which is the potential to gain further discriminating power, as she has been too naive in the past. The disguise of her father's clothes suggests she has to set out with the persona given to her by him. Night comes and she climbs into a tree, which bears white flowers. A tree is the symbol of the self, and the white flowers relate to the feminine reinforcing the notion of becoming in touch with her feminine nature as she is now out in Mother Nature.

At midnight, three ducks appear. Midnight is thought to be the moment at which the presence of God appears and disperses evil spirits.[194] It is a time when she has to face her own inner demons and learn the secret to become more in touch with her self.

The three witches disguised now as ducks actually tempt her toward consciousness, a challenge to be back in relationship with her animus. Ducks are animals that can go from land to water to air, and thus a very important symbol, and these ducks are wallowing in the ashes in front of a fire, suggesting some kind of transformation is needed. There is energy there with the symbol of the fire and hence the girl now has a choice to live in connection with her self and to create energy toward life. Since the three witches were transformed into ducks, this may suggest the ducks in this tale are a feminine symbol, and thus, it is from the feminine she has to learn the secret that will allow her to be in true relationship.

The same kind of polarity exists in the archetype of the mother here. This archetype has positive and negative sides and thus has to be transformed, and this is connected with the sacrifice of the negative energy. She transforms this destructive energy into the remedy. Specifically, she has to slay the three witches, and it is from their blood that the remedy is found. That is, she has to sacrifice a negative attitude to reach the healing aspect. This is done with the help of God, *Deo concedente*, which Jung mentioned in *Psychology and Alchemy*, saying, "We are told that a man can receive the secret knowledge only through divine inspiration or from the lips of a master, and also that no one can complete the work except with the help of God."[195] This is not just to maintain ego power but also to be in relationship between the ego and the self.

As an orphan, she is vulnerable and receptive to the unconscious, and if she can be receptive then she has the possibility to embark on an individuation process. The orphan is more alone compared to others so not the same inner parent would develop when one is in relationship with a real mother and a real father. That is, there is not the guidance and direction or even lack of this given and hence one is called early to

194 G. Jobes, *Dictionary of Mythology Folklore and Symbols, Part 2*.
195 Jung, Religious Ideas in Alchemy, *Psychology and Alchemy, CW 12*, ¶ 450.

rely on oneself or to seek out a substitute. Buddha had a supernatural mother and Mohammed was an orphan as mentioned in Chapter 4. She is an orphan and, like Moses, is called to the possibility of an individuation process.

The secret she learns is that there must be a sacrifice of her one-sided logos way of life, as evidenced by the expectation she had for the man to show up and be there if she fulfilled her duty to fill the water bowl daily. How often it is so easy to expect a partner to fulfill one's needs if we do what we think is needed, but this does not allow for the feelings of the other. Her life was lacking Eros and he brings her the erotic life, but she has to grow up to be a mature woman. However, he is a ghost lover, a shadow lover. If a woman has a ghost lover, she is possessed by a spirit that is not coming to life, and to be fully in life she has to be in contact with a real man not just a spiritual lover. This is the difficulty of falling in love with a person who is not fully emotionally available; there is not the possibility for a truly intimate relationship with the other.

It is important to ask the following questions: What is so fascinating about that person? What do I love so much about this person? It is important to know what part of one's self is being seen or heard in the other person, and the question becomes, "Do I have this part also?" The answer, if we are honest, is that there is a part of oneself not lived out enough, and the solution becomes how we make that part come alive. This is something that must be done alone, and one needs to give up placing demands on the other person which must be honored by one's self. The idea is to see clearly what he or she is in you. We learn by seeing the partner only as a human being, not a god. Of course, the other mystery is also necessary; that is, to see the god or goddess in the other. Essentially, there needs to be a balance between the archetype and the profane, the person in reality with what we project onto him or her.

The healing comes with a feather. The feather to heal the wounds is a part of intuition that is in touch with the wounded spirit within her. This is how to deal with the negative mother. This fine intuition must not be too rough and hence the symbol of the feather. The soul is fragile and there should be no power complex involved here. Thus, it is not the ego which is doing it, but the feather represents something sensitive in the unconscious that is doing the healing. She must give much life energy to rescuing her inner prince; it is the transformation of a complex that is going on.

Now she stops to rest and again the number three appears as time, again a dynamic that something needs to be made conscious. She now learns how very ill the prince is and thus with the help of the old man, an old father archetype that helps her spiritually, and the developing inner masculine, she rushes off to the palace.

The coat suggests she has to disguise herself with the authority of the father. So still disguised as an old man, she is let into the palace, but she tells everyone to leave them alone while she ministers to the prince. This healing needs to be done with care, and now there develops a positive relationship to the wounded animus through this caring.

After the healing she does not admit to loving the prince. It is a secret that needs to remain a secret because it needs protection and needs time to develop. If one is evolving and changing then one needs some protection to allow for time for this development. If you tell others you are on this path, it can bring forth jealousy and envy and then you are not appreciated for the essence of the individuation. This process has to be in the *vas Hermeticum*: not laid open to the public or laid open to the mother complex.

The orphan does not take the reward to live in the palace, but instead takes a ring from the queen and a ring from the prince. The rings symbolize an undifferentiated wholeness, which still needs to be connected to someone. She still is not linked with the prince and so she goes home to wait. For the prince still has some work to do himself. He comes after her with revenge for what he has perceived her to have done to him, which suggests that he too has a negative mother complex. It is not until he recognizes her for who she is and not for the devouring mother he thought her to be that a true relationship can occur. Once recognized for who they truly are, not for what they thought the other was, can they be united in marriage.

Summary

The culmination of the little orphan girl's journey is the realization that she is part of a divine plan. It takes time to find this out. The death of her mother, the feminine, leaves her and her father with a great hole at the center of their existence. Then the death of the father leaves her naively to deal with the world. The final task of her journey is to see that hole and naiveté, not as an empty void, but as a potential universe. She has to learn to trust the darkness of the night, and she has to follow her own feelings in the silence of her own soul, allowing herself to be guided from inside rather than charging toward conscious ideals; the feminine gradually becomes conscious and is manifested in an authentic relationship to an Other. Trusting a feminine order opens her to the totally irrational and totally new. Her relationship to that otherness, to her animus, releases her creativity.

With the death of her parents, she had to leave the unconscious Garden of Eden. Had she become married at this point, her existence would be empty because none of her personal life would have been lived; there would have been no connection to her own creativity. Jung said, "Fear of fate is a very understandable phenomenon, for it is incalculable, immeasurable, full of unknown dangers. But anyone who refuses to experience life must stifle his desire to live."[196]

The orphan is called to go on such a journey, but she needs a strong enough ego that can dialogue with the unconscious. The tale again confirms a calling to individuate for the orphan. She had to leave a predictable, but deadening pattern and open herself to possibility. She had to remain hidden in her father's clothes until she could sort through what belonged to her and what did not until she recognized her own spirit stirring within her. She chose with caring and tenderness to care for that wounded part of her and to wait with patience to find the meaning within herself. The covenant with the inner masculine gave her a firm standpoint and then she could be more grounded in her own feelings and body. Thus, she was no longer bound to the rigid world of her parental complexes.

---

196 Jung, The Song of the Moth, *Symbols, CW 5,* ¶ 165.

Jung said, "Not only is it [to individuate] desirable, it is absolutely indispensable because, through his contamination with others, he falls into situations and commits actions which bring him into disharmony with himself." That is, he or she acts in a way contrary to his nature and thus "a man [or woman] can neither be at one with himself nor accept responsibility for himself."[197] For the orphan, no longer being held to these parental complexes, having patience to complete the integration of the masculine and feminine from within, and valuing the uniqueness in the other is a hero's journey.

This tale is universal and found in many cultures. It seems to speak to the feminine compensation for a patriarchal culture, that is, a transformation of a patriarchal collective attitude; specifically, toward a transformation that is more related and has the feminine feeling values. This continues to be present in many cultures today.

Up to this point we have looked at the historical context of the orphan, the psychological orphan, the orphan as a symbol, and the orphan in a fairy tale. The orphan is alone and yet potentially is called to a greater development. How can the orphan be at one within herself and in her world?

---

197 Jung, The Relations Between the Ego and the Unconscious, *Two Essays on Analytical Psychology,* CW 7, ¶ 373.

Chapter 6

THE ORPHAN AS AN ARCHETYPE AND COMPLEX

> As a numinous factor, the archetype determines the nature
> of the configurational process and the course it will follow,
> with seeming fore-knowledge, or as though it were already
> in possession of the goal to be circumscribed by the centring
> process.
>
> C.G. Jung[198]

The feeling of being alone in the world is multifaceted. These experiences can include being a literal orphan, a child without parents; the feeling of being an orphan, a child with parents; and/or being compelled for whatever reasons to be in the process of becoming whole, of becoming an individual, thus, a journey to be taken alone. In addition, the archetype can be activated for no apparent reason. We have seen how the cultural context may provide the stimulus for activation of the orphan complex, or provide the means by which the archetype may be known and how the personal experiences may lead to the feeling of being an orphan. And when there are many of these signs we can no longer ignore them. Are we at this point now? In our technological world are we

---

198 Jung, On the Nature of the Psyche. *The Structure and Dynamics of the Psyche, CW 8,* ¶ 411.

neglecting human contact for virtual relationships and hence the need for a counter-balance?

The activation of the orphan complex suggests a calling to go further, to look at one's life and to hold the potential for developing wholeness. This is not contrary to the individuation process, but one way in which one is called to this journey.

Jung thought that the only way one could know about the unconscious was through complexes, "the living units of the unconscious psyche." Unlike Freud, who thought the *via regia,* royal road, to the unconscious was the dream, Jung thought it was the complex, "which is the architect of dreams and of symptoms."[199] The complex has an archetypal core emanating from the collective unconscious, and it may also arise autonomously.

The orphan may come out of a state familiar to the culture of the times, but also is entered in part due to living one's destiny or fate. "As the archetypes…are relatively autonomous, they cannot be integrated simply by rational means…but require a real coming to terms with them…."[200] Jung emphasized knowing one's standpoint and keeping it "…firmly anchored to the earth…"[201] before venturing into the collective unconscious. The personal work may be of utmost importance to ground the individual and hence the importance of understanding the psychological orphan and giving preference to personal material in the beginning of the work.

The orphan complex may result from the interactive or, better yet, relational milieu and out of inadequate or disrupted attachment to the mother resulting in an early wounding. In addition, there is a certain fate that becomes constellated when this particular mother and this particular infant are in contact with each other. In some ways the mother is "the exponent of fate, [which is] one of the great tragedies of being a mother."[202] Thus, the activation of the complex may be a reaction to one's individual experience. This will be illustrated later in the chapter.

---

199 Jung, A Review of Complex Theory, *The Structure and Dynamics of the Psyche, CW 8,* ¶ 210.

200 Jung, *The Archetypes of the Collective Unconscious, CW 9i,* ¶ 85.

201 Jung, *Archetypes of the Collective Unconscious, CW 9i,* ¶ 51.

202 Kathrin Asper, personal communication, April 5, 2001.

However, this is not the only means by which a complex, which has an archetypal core, may be activated.

Jung stated, "There are as many archetypes as there are typical situations in life." At first these images are forms without context representing the possibility of a certain kind of perception and action. "When a situation occurs which corresponds to a given archetype, that archetype becomes activated...."[203] In one of Jung's last letters, he stated, "Archetypes are forms of different aspects expressing the creative psychic background. They are and therefore always have been numinous and therefore 'divine.' In a very generalizing way one can therefore define them as attributes of the creator."[204]

Moreover, von Franz discusses the importance of the changes in the zeitgeist, which are based on creative processes in the collective unconscious. The events of the day are merely subsumed under the direction of the collective unconscious. Here "...the spontaneous transformation of the symbol of the Self (that is, of the god-man and the God image of every period of history) has played a role in structuring historical events...."[205] We can understand this as a reality that may be ruled by destiny, law or meaning. In order to illustrate this, a story from the *Bhagavad-Gita* will be recounted.

The *Bhagavad-Gita* illustrates the moral crisis faced between living an individual life to living a life that sustains the moral order of the cosmos, society and the individual. This sacred text is located within the *Mahabharata*, an Indian war epic. The context is Hinduism in which right and wrong are not absolute and are decided on by the relativity of values and obligations.[206]

The *Gita's* main theme revolves around a feud over succession to the ancient kingdom of Kurukshetra in northern India. There is a battle between two sets of cousins and this is where the poem begins. Arjuna, the one cousin's younger brother is about to begin the battle, but his heart sinks at the prospect of the thought of slaughter of many of those

203 Jung, The Concept of the Collective Unconscious, *Archetypes, CW 9i,* ¶ 99.
204 Adler & Jaffe, *C.G. Jung Letters, Volume 2*, p. 606.
205 von Franz, *Archetypal Dimensions*, pp. 263-4.
206 B. Miller, *The Bhagavad-Gita*.

who are nearest and dearest to him and yet are on the other side. Krishna, an incarnation of Vishnu, is Arjuna's guide and his main purpose is to persuade Arjuna to go into battle with a clear conscious.

Krishna begins with arguments that you cannot kill the soul even though you may kill the body because it is eternal, and since the soul of a warrior slain in battle goes straight to heaven, he is really doing a service to his kinsman in ridding them of their bodies. Then he goes on to say refusing to fight would be violating the *dharma* of his caste; and lastly he would be accused by his enemies of having opted out of the war because he was afraid. If he goes through with the battle he cannot lose. He will be killed, in which case he will go straight to heaven, or he will conquer in which case he will inherit the earth.

Arjuna is not interested in these arguments. So Krishna instructs him on how final liberation can be won even by a warrior engaged in battle. This can be achieved by a total dissociation of one's self, which is eternal and therefore not responsible for acts committed in time, from acts performed by a temporal body. The goal is for the soul to enter its timeless nature.

Thus, the hero embodies order and sacred duty-*dharma*, and the opponents embody chaos—*adharma*. Heroism is really to fulfill one's dharma, "...which may involve extraordinary forms of sacrifice, penance, devotion to a divine authority, and spiritual victory over evil...."[207] While it is a battle, which Arjuna fights, it is also representative of the state of mind of Arjuna's inner conflict. How can he kill family and feel good about this? Ultimately, Arjuna comes into dialogue with Krishna, a god who commands devotion, and Arjuna comes to see himself mirrored in the divine. This takes Arjuna to an awareness beyond the personal and social values and to recognize he must live his destiny in order to be authentic; true to his part in the larger picture. This is so difficult to do when one feels the pull of the collective values, but essential if we are to live a life with consciousness. In this poem the death is that of the body, however in reality the death may not be a literal death, but a psychological letting go and moving on.

---

207 Miller, *The Bhagavad-Gita*, p. 3.

Like Jung, the *Gita* is encouraging of living the experience not just having a belief that one must accept. The god is revealed to Arjuna only through devotion, which allows for a resolution of the conflict between the worldly life of duties and giving one's life to something larger. What Arjuna sees is the majestic order of the cosmos, which includes destructiveness and the realization that his duty to fight is ultimately linked to Krishna's divine activity. In the following, Krishna reveals his terrifying identity as creator and destroyer of everything in the universe:

> I am time grown old,
> creating world destruction,
> set in motion
> to annihilate the worlds;
> even without you,
> all these warriors
> arrayed in hostile ranks
> will cease to exist.
>
> Therefore, arise
> and win glory!
> Conquer your foes
> and fulfill your kingship!
> They are already
> slain by me.
> Be just my instrument,
> the archer at my side![208]

Through the dialogue in the poem, it is apparent that it is not an easy task to follow one's dharma or as Jung says to go on the individuation path. In fact, Jung states, "And I told you in that connection that it was impossible for us to contain the whole of our psychology within ourselves; it is quite inevitable that certain parts will always be projected. That is the reason why we need other human beings, why we need objects; life makes no sense if completely detached, we are only complete

---

208 Miller, *The Bhagavad-Gita*, pp. 103-4.

in a community or in a relationship."[209] For the person with an orphan complex, it means that one must foster relationship in order for further development to occur.

Andreas Schweizer, Jungian Analyst, has likened the inner-psychic experience of the archetype to a psychic earthquake, which comes out of the blue, with the resultant feeling of being completely alone or abandoned. And whoever has to experience such a shock must become creative in his or her life. If not, one pays with a huge neurosis.[210]

The following gives description to the experience of an orphan complex followed by more elaborate stories of the orphan complex.

The Experience of the Orphan

This feeling of being an orphan, *orphanus sum*, even when the parents have been present, is seen in the following reflections of a 47-year-old now parentless, childless woman. Although she was married, she experienced feeling alone in the world. She had two parents growing up, but her mother returned to work when she was 6 weeks old, and most pertinent to our discussion is that the mother felt resentful toward her husband who was no longer exclusively devoted to her after the birth of the child. This can be a typical feeling when a baby comes into the couple relationship, but because the couple could not discuss this, the mother's feelings remained unconscious and had subsequent consequences for the mother-infant communication. As a result the child most likely never felt she had her mother's unconditional love. This woman described the feeling of being alone in the world as follows:

> I am not lonely, but I am alone. I want someone to be near, but I do not want to have to give anything or to have any demands put on me. The presence of another is important to me. However, when I am with friends or colleagues or relatives, I experience them as not really seeing me. I am angry and irritable on the inside although I do not show it to them because I fear cutting off the potential that they will give to

---

209 C. Douglas, *Visions*, p 1367.
210 Schweizer, Personal communication, September 9, 2010.

me in a way that I need. But I do not know what that way is, I just know for now nothing feels right. When I have a conversation with these others, I leave feeling empty. Why did I bother to interact with such a person, I am not the better for it, nor, most likely, either are they. In fact, why do they even want to interact with me in the first place? If they could see my real thoughts about them, they would certainly want to avoid me. This feeling of being so alone in the world is pervasive, I cannot shake it, and it is always with me.

I am a stranger to others around me, even though I may have lived with them for years, or gone through very intense experiences with them. I am always on the lookout for the ultimate interaction, the one that will feed me and give to me what I so desire. I cannot cut off any potentialities and therefore find myself doing things that perhaps I would not have done if I were not driven by the potentiality of obtaining something that will sustain me and turn this feeling around.

However, what I do is to interact on a superficial level, it is nice, it appears to be understanding, I smile and all seems to be well. I think in the back of my mind that there is a possibility that I will feel better if I am with this person or, perhaps, they will have something to say or do that make me feel better. But even though they are giving to me it is not enough. From my perspective, the interaction is a pretense and the anger grows within me. The feeling remains and the irritability and anger do not leave me. I want to cry, but there will be no one to hear my tears or to understand how I really feel. I am inconsolable. I am so alone.

Her longing is real and she suffers in her desire for a close relationship with another. She has over the years expected that someone else will fill the void, but she was always disappointed in relationships, choosing weak men who could not at least fight back with her so she would have to realize that her expectations were unrealistic.

What she does not yet understand is that there is a force within her that is moving her towards wholeness, she wants to rely on another, but in fact she must acknowledge and rely on herself and on the Self for direction in her life.

Personal Stories

In order to more fully explore the archetype of the orphan, two individuals are discussed, an adult and a child. The importance of this discussion is to further understand the orphan and how this can be manifest in the history and in the working relationship with the therapist since these may be preverbal memories. While the adult and the child presented with depressive symptoms, the orphan was identified with the complex and archetype manifested in the analytic work.

A Middle-Aged Man

Mr. S. is a 39-year-old scientist who reported that every so often he goes into a "slump" and needs someone to talk to. That is, he experiences low energy to accomplishing tasks and yet when he can talk with someone who is understanding he feels better. He is aware that he has mood swings and has recently been mildly depressed and unable to complete work projects, instead spending his time, for example, watching movies or organizing his work to the extent that the larger projects become delayed and he barely meets deadlines. Moreover, he reported experiencing relationship difficulties with his wife. He finds most everything she does annoying and, although he cares for her, he stated he has never loved her. When he married her, he primarily felt sorry for her because of a recent death in her family. In addition, at the time he was making a move to a new job location and it would not make sense for her to accompany him unless they were to marry. He stated he is not lonely, but is alone with his thoughts and feelings. He considered divorce, but does not want to be alone, saying that the marriage gave him a kind of security.

Mr. S. was adopted when he was 3 months of age after a brief time with a foster mother; the adoptive mother was 45 years old at the time of the adoption. He recalls his adoptive mother always telling him how much he meant to her coming into her life. He was informed of his adoptive status when he was age 6 and recalled no difficulties with this, but had fantasies of figuring out his genealogical roots.

Mr. S. is very fond of his adoptive mother and had a belief that she was a good mother. However, he related that he became more aware of his mother's discomfort around babies and hence around him when he observed her with his younger adoptive sister's children. There she was tentative and not very interactive on a physical level. His adoptive father corroborated this story, elaborating that this was how she was with him and his sister when they were babies.

Mr. S. searched for his biological mother and found her a few years ago. She was hoping he would contact her and was delighted to hear from him. She told him, "I am getting to know the son I never knew." He learned he was given up for adoption because the pregnancy was out of wedlock, and his maternal grandmother would not allow her daughter to keep the baby, even though she was in her mid-20s at the time. This grandmother died prior to him making contact with his biological mother. He now limits his contact with her because she is so "gloomy" and her idealistic thoughts about him make him feel uncomfortable.

From this brief history, there are several factors to be taken into account. He comes in stating he has been feeling depressed, but the quality of the depression is around wanting to be connected with another who will understand him and alleviate this depression. He does not feel understood by his wife whom he married out of a sense of obligation and feelings of empathy about her loss. He could articulate his feelings of being alone and of not being understood and his longing for this, which seemingly was projected onto his wife.

Of course, Mr. S. cannot remember his relationship with his mother as an infant, but he had two mothers who, by his report, idealized him and were so very grateful that he was in their lives. He had the following dream after the initial appointment was made and prior to our first meeting.

> There were two clans that were feuding. One was Serbian and the other maybe Greek. The head of the Serbians was in his 30's and very dark and hairy. I was afraid of offending some kind of Mafia code. But for some reason, and apparently with his knowledge and permission, his wife was available to me.

> She was very Mediterranean looking, sturdy and game, warm,
> seeming a little older than me.

Mr. S. stated the woman in the dream looked like his biological mother, who he elaborated had a close resemblance to Frida Kahlo, artist. The Serbians were killing and their reasons were rational but made no sense. The two tribes described in his dream seemed to relate to the split between his adoptive and biological families, which for him represented emotional turmoil, perhaps rational, but not making any sense. The woman in the dream is sexually charged and available to him, but emotionally disturbed on some level given his association to Kahlo, who in reality was physically and emotionally traumatized.

From this initial dream I became aware of a struggle within him about his origins and the feelings with which he presented himself to the analysis. There was a split in him about the two families he had, and this was life threatening as he was afraid of offending an unknown code. What could this code be? Does it have something to do with his orphan beginnings? Nevertheless, the man makes his wife available to him and she serves to be the bridge to his unconscious. The dream presented a manipulative, seductive female figure that could be frightening to him.

Mr. S. expressed feeling as if no one understood him and, in truth, he did not reveal very much of himself to others. When talking about relationships with significant others he described something "gray" with a feeling that he was "unloved." As previously noted, I came to understand that his mother was not very comfortable with babies and did not hold or engage easily with him although she was delighted to have him in her life. I had an image of an infant who now is experiencing his third mother within the space of a few months and is not able to fully engage with her and to be understood in his longings to be close. Kohut[211] described the importance of the visual area, as did Schore,[212] and stated that if the mother recoils from the child's body then visual or other senses can be hyper-cathected in order to substitute for the failures that occurred in physical closeness within the relationship. This was true for

---

211 H. Kohut, *The Analysis of the Self: A Systematic Approach to the Psychoanalytic Treatment of Narcissistic Personality Disorders.*

212 A.N. Schore, *Affect Regulation and the Origin of the Self.*

this man, who stated he attempted to be physically close to his wife, but she limited his touch and explicating how it was to be done frustrated him. Thus, Mr. S. ultimately married a woman (his projected anima) who frustrated him in a similar way as he experienced growing up. He longs to be close but instead must compartmentalize his feelings. I could imagine that if one were too distanced emotionally from him he would fall into despair and yet if one were too close, he would experience it as symbiotic in nature and also unsatisfying.

How does one assist an analysand for whom the feeling of orphan becomes constellated? As previously stated, one cannot become too close too quickly and one cannot be abandoning, and this fine balance needs to have an open dialogue as no analyst, like no mother, can be perfectly attuned to all needs at all times. For me, letting the analysand know in the beginning that our relationship needs to be a dialogue about which we can talk was important. He later could tell me that this addressed the issue of being in relationship for him and that it mattered that I cared enough to tell him we would need to talk about our relationship.

Regardless, his feelings of being alone in the world manifested in his inability to divorce a woman for whom he had no love and on some level, disgust. That in itself was not a reason to think the orphan was being constellated, but his stated fear that there would be no one there for him was overwhelming, and his emphasis on needing to be understood and valued was what drove him in the relationship. It was as if he continued to try and work through how to emotionally relate to his wife in the hope that she would be responsive to him, but instead he continued to play out the same abandoning pattern. That is, his wife idealized him on some level, and in their relationship he had compartmentalized his feelings, now specifically by having no sexual contact with her. Having no physical contact in this way eliminated the possibility of being rejected by her, which had been their previous pattern and now made him feel as if he was an orphan. This was not to say he married someone like his mother, but because none of this has been made conscious, he continued to repeat similar patterns.

The difficulty with relating to woman, the imprint of the negative mother imago, and the importance of that early touch which had been wounded is seen in the following dream:

> There was a device that allowed several people to be trans-ported to Mars in a kind of frame where their heads were embedded. They could talk to one another in their narrowed sidelined state and see out to observe the environment. Due to technical advances, one or two could now be transport-ed bodily, but their hands had to be removed and replaced with metal pincers. As a result, two who had fallen in love could now regard each other face to face for the first time. The woman's head was still embedded in the frame: dark hair, whitened, shiny skin, and red lipstick. A pearly or china-doll look, but smiling. Then a further advance allowed the hands to be shipped and reattached. They had to be delivered in good time to prevent decay, but someone was blocking them administratively. I asked who was behind this and a mysteri-ous, breathy voice answered: "I want to hurt them." I awoke from the nightmare crying out in a thick voice, "Who wants to hurt them?"

The dream was terrifying for this man. One can see how in some ways there is a fragmented chaos around trying to relate to a significant other. He wanted to relate, but he was thwarted and this became life threatening for these beings. Of importance was the loving gaze and then the next more intimate contact would be through touch and the potential for this was being blocked. His dream shows the body and mind split within him.

The transference has been important in that this man needed to feel validated and understood, but too much of that would also be frighten-ing to him. He could understand having to fight for his life to relate and he continued to do this with a woman who was not able to be there in an intimate way. On the one hand he wanted her to respond, but on the other hand if she did, that would be anxiety producing to him. Thus, there needed to be a balance between the two of holding and setting appropriate boundaries so he could trust the space to reveal himself. Heretofore, he has counteracted the subjectively painful feeling of self-fragmentation by a variety of forced actions, such as his excessive work or over organization. These compensatory structures were what he must work through therapeutically in order for him to be in more intimate relationships. Staying on the personal level aided this man to become more grounded. Once he experienced this, he was able to become in touch with his creativity and destiny to further new theories within his scientific field.

A Latency-Aged Child

The constellation of the orphan can also be seen in the story of a child who has two parents. This can occur when there has been a significant disruption in the mother-child attachment or there has been some physical problem or environmental disruption, and/or there has been a lack of resonance in the mother-infant dyad. The boy in this case can articulate feeling very alone and completely misunderstood.

John, as I call him, is an 11-year-old boy who was brought for therapy by his parents because of increased negativity about his school, difficulty taking instruction, and difficulty doing group work. He is a perfectionist and has trouble working with others. He often feels different from his peers because of his interests and his inability to relate to them. It is easier for him to talk with adults, and one often thinks of him as a much older child than his stated chronological age.

The initial evaluation with John revealed he was depressed. This was discussed with his parents who elected not to follow through with the recommendation for therapy until 6 months later when he began talking about committing suicide. The school insisted he be taken to therapy, although the parents minimized that he would have actually followed through on these threats and were quite directive in their comments to him that they did not want to ever hear this kind of talk again. The image of the happy family had been broken in the parents' eyes.

When John was 6 weeks of age the parents moved to a foreign country. The father spoke the language and the mother had to learn the language, but both were looking forward to this move. The father liked his work and the mother made friends with her neighbors who also had small children; she joined a social organization from her country of origin.

John's birth history was unremarkable, and he was described as an easy baby, but he always had difficulty sleeping through the night, which necessitated the mother having to lie down with him until he fell asleep or be with him if he woke up in the middle of the night. This continued until age 3. Developmental milestones were achieved within normal limits. As a toddler he was easily frustrated, liked things orderly, and had "intense" temper tantrums. When he was 2 years 7 months of age the maternal grandfather died; this was a difficult time for the mother, although she minimized that this interfered with her parenting. The mother could not attend her father's funeral due to the late stages of her second pregnancy and, thus, being unable to fly on an airplane. The father reflected that she cried a lot and saw their son acting tenderly toward his mother. At 2 years 8 months his brother was born, but again the parents stated there were no difficulties with this.

When John entered school, he was very active and had difficulty keeping focused. He was placed in a classroom with fewer students and he improved. Throughout his schooling he maintained loyalty to certain teachers and, in fact, was rude to a substitute teacher when she tried to do things differently than the regular teacher. He expected conformity to what he perceived to be the cultural rules of the school environment, and he was going to make sure others complied with these rules.

Nevertheless, this family seemed to have a history without any significant problems, but yet there was John who was now voicing suicidal threats and feeling so alienated from himself and others. What could possibly be going on with him?

Kathrin Asper[213] talked about emotional abandonment by the parent in which the child does not receive good-enough mothering, a concept first developed by Winnicott.[214] This type of abandonment is experienced when the child does not have his feelings noticed or understood with

---

213 K. Asper, *The Abandoned Child Within: On Losing and Regaining Self-Worth.*

214 J. Abram, *The Language of Winnicott: A Dictionary and Guide to Understanding his Work.*

empathy by someone else. This reminds us of the example Ainsworth made in observing the Ugandan mother who was physically present to her child, but emotionally abandoning not because by all standards she was a bad mother, but because she was very stressed by other pressures and not emotionally present. This seemed to be the case with John, and the problems were manifested early in his irritability and overcompensation for orderliness. He wanted more from his mother, and his inability to sleep and nighttime waking expressed his need to be closer to her and for her to be more affectively attuned to him. For all practical purposes, it was difficult to understand what the pressures were for this mother, but most significant was her minimizing of her son's emotional needs and her defensiveness that she was not the best mother to him. This speaks, perhaps, to her own wounding that she needed to protect and not be seen by others as having any problems, but also she was doing her very best given her own grieving for her deceased father. Certainly these parents resisted professional help, even for their son's serious emotional problems. They eventually turned to therapy only because of increasing pressure from the school.

These parents had tried, like so many of us, to allay John's feelings of being different and the teasing of other children by comforting him and telling him he was all right. This well-intentioned support is emotionally abandoning because it does not recognize his shame, humiliation, and despair. This is when it is important to stay with his feelings, to notice them and to share them openly. It is during these times that the feeling of the orphan can be recognized and then we do not feel so alone in the world. This has been the healing process for John in the analysis.

For several months John could do nothing but talk about the unfairness with which he felt the other children treated him and how mean they were to him. He would report incidents of how he was not respected, but he could not see how he did not respect others. John wrote a story called "Just Plain Mean" about an incident at school, which he described as "probably one of the toughest days in my life." This related to being called names by some other boys who took his ball and threw it in the mud and, from his perspective, kept bullying him throughout the day. Finally, he threw a ball at one of them that hit a boy in the head, who then tearfully went to the teacher and received sympathy and

John got in trouble. He summed this up by saying, "I felt miserable and angry. I felt like the whole world had turned its back on me."

At times during the analysis, he would be within a few inches of my face to tell me these stories; he needed my undivided attention. This was in contrast to the beginning in which he typically did not look at me directly. As he was listened to and validated for his feelings, he began to be able to see that he could not change the other children, but that perhaps something in him could be changed.

His ability to see this came when he told a story about being on the bus with his class and how some children were listening to music and he was annoyed by the "noise." He challenged them, stating he had a right to have silence, but then he was unmercifully teased and in trouble by the teacher for causing such a fuss. He told the story and once validated for his civil liberties, I wondered out loud if these children had a right to listen to music as well. He was now at a point where he could hear they, too, had a need and it was his attitude that needed to change. This change and his ability to see this came through an empathic listening/understanding for many months and through his sandplay work.

John made two sandtrays when we began our work together. The first sandtray he called "Times Square," a favorite place in New York City where he stated the family would often take visitors; he then quickly erased it and made the next tray. This first tray was devoid of any objects, it was like a map and one had a perspective view from above looking down. This was a familiar scene and one that had pleasant memories for him. He was bringing back a happy memory to now what he experienced as a life devoid of anything happy. He told how his family took visitors to a very glitzy part of America; it was filled with actors and plays and was not very relational. I wondered could this be part of his experience of lacking emotional connection on a deeper level. However, the appearance of a map was showing me his experience and the possibility for change (Figure 17). The second sand tray he spontaneously titled, "A Sandy Christmas," and he told a story about a war with soldiers, "good guys" against the "bullies," who were being captured and buried in the snow. He disguised himself as the Eiffel tower at one point. He builds tunnels to the houses where he could be protected (Figure 18). Now he must begin the fight a real hero's journey.

John was letting me know about his inner conflicts within his family as well as the outer conflicts with his peers. His depression was a way to let others know that it had all become too much for him; specifically that the compensation of doing things rationally was becoming too one-sided. There were many aggressive impulses and it was difficult to contain them any longer. He could find a place to be, the houses that were containing and safe, and that he needed to be detached from the conflict. He needed to be in a place where he could bring peace to these inner and outer battles. The Eiffel tower was seen as a male symbol and his wish to be admired and viewed from all sides, specifically to be seen and valued.

Figure 17. Times square. Source: Photo by A.F. Punnett

Figures 18a & 18b. A Sandy Christmas & close-up.
Source: Photo by A.F. Punnett, 2000.

The process with John was over a 16-month period and there were 51 sandtrays. He completed a tray in every session except one. There was a time when the parents thought he was doing so well that it would be time to stop and told him, unbeknown to me, that this would be his last meeting. During this session he made 10 trays trying to complete his process. Fortunately, the parents were willing to have him continue, albeit on a monthly basis for another six months. During these last six month, John went very deeply in his sandplay work touching archetypal contents and then his last tray was of a peaceful park scene.

This process yielded remarkable results within a relatively short time, with much improvement in the presenting problems. And as a result of the therapy, he was able to be a contributor in his academic environment and to have a playful balance with his peers.

Further Thoughts

The orphan as an archetype and complex were explored in this chapter. While there can be personal, experiential reasons for the orphan to appear one must also remember that the archetype can come spontaneously through creative processes in the collective unconscious. This is especially evident in the epic poem of the *Bhagavad-Gita*. One must always be aware, that the archetype is never directly experienced and therefore is numinous and can "emerge from an individual experience, but this does not necessarily mean that it has to emerge from a personal event like an abuse or abandonment. It can emerge from an inner-psychic event, which activates the complex and creates the respective archetypal image."[215] In addition, two personal stories illustrated the feeling of being alone related to wanting to be understood and seen not only for our accomplishments, but also for our struggles and suffering, which free one to be in touch with creative processes.

Both of these cases were males, which were intentionally presented to highlight the importance of the acquisition of the feminine principle. That is, to be in touch with feelings and moods, pay attention to intuitions and receptiveness to the irrational, have a capacity of personal love

---

215 Schweizer, personal communication, September 9, 2010.

and a feeling for nature and lastly to be related to the unconscious.[216]
This is the way of the feminine, the yin. The Way in Taoist terms is to
restore the original God-given spirit.[217] Of course, this is always an ebb
and flow, a balancing and need for both, as described by Sun Bu-er:[218]

> The beginning of the sustenance of life
> Is all in yin and yang.
> The limitless can open up
> The light of the great limit.
> Diligently polished, the mirror of mind
> Is bright as the moon;
> The universe in a grain
> May rise, or it may hide.

Zhou Xuanjing[219] describes the receptive as "…the mother sign of the
I Ching," and that when one practices, meditation is not about being
quiet but rather the meditation "…is a technique for clearing the mind
so as to release positive energy from the prison of mental habits."

Whenever we turn to images from the soul, Schweizer contends "we
are obliged to penetrate psychologically into the preconscious totality
of the collective unconscious, leaving behind the domain of merely personal psychology." This is to look beyond the personal story, whether
good or bad, and look at the context within "…the entire cosmos and
the human beings embedded within it."[220]

Around 1500 BC in Egypt, the split between the individual and the
objective world was non-existent. Nature was considered something
real, was created by the Sungod, and the individual was in one with
this and also fearful of being separated from the gods, hence paying
them homage even in the afterlife. This was to connect the life force
with the body of the deceased in order to guarantee future protection of
the deceased by his soul. Interestingly, in those times, the feminine was

---

216 Jung, von Franz, Henderson, Jacobi & Jaffe, *Man and His Symbols*.
217 T. Cleary, *The Taoist Classics, Volume 3*.
218 T. Cleary, *Immortal Sisters: Secret Teachings of Taoist Women*, p. 75.
219 Cleary, *Immortal Sisters*, p. 71.
220 Schweizer, *Sungod's Journey*, p. 12.

related to the sky because the realm of ideas and intellectual concepts were an emotional experience in contrast to Western culture where ideas are related to scientific investigation. In those times, the individual was connected with the totality. Now we study Nature as if it were separate from us. Nevertheless, the point is that we may be touched by various archetypes, perhaps the orphan, and it is important to subordinate one's own will and knowledge to an inner truth and law that far transcend ego-consciousness.[221] This is the necessary aloneness that can nurture and propel our individuation process.

The personal feeling of being alone is a kind of abandonment, but what is prominent is the feeling of not being valued in relational moments. This may also be an inner-psychic experience in the revelation or experience of the dark side of god, as it were.[222] The Other may be there, but not present in ways that bring meaning to the child or any orphan. Thus, the feminine or the relationship is not present and, yet, what is needed.

---

221 Schweizer, *Sungod's Journey.*
222 Schweizer, personal communication, September 9, 2010.

Chapter 7

RECONNECTING:
ALONE YET AT ONE WITH THE WORLD

>...if one advances confidently in the direction of his dreams,
>and endeavors to live the life which he has imagined, he will
>meet with a success unexpected in common hours. ...and he
>will live with the license of a higher order of beings.
>
>H.D. Thoreau[223]

When the orphan within us is activated, there is an opportunity to stay
with it and discover its meaning for our life. It is not an easy task, but an
important one if we are to be in touch with our true nature.

All Alone – At One

The following series of pictures from the Bridgeman Art Library in London illustrate this process of being an orphan to being at one with oneself and the world.

"The Orphan" by Pierre Roch shows the empty bed, a place of rest but also a place where life is conceived, it is now devoid of all life as one sees in the background the horse-drawn hearse taking the parent or parents to their final resting place (Figure 19). Von Franz spoke of the

---

223 H. D. Thoreau, *Walden or Life in the Woods*, p. 356.

Figure 19. The Orphan or Fatal Cholera by Pierre Roch Vigneron.
Source: Bridgeman Art Library. Reprinted by permission.

bed as "a place of *abaissement de niveau mental*, where you connect
with your unconscious, with your instincts and with your body."[224] She
went on to say; "the bed is where all instinctual life fulfills itself—birth,
death, lovemaking, where we get in touch with our instincts and with
the unconscious."[225] To the right is a child, a potential for the future is
depicted, but she is alone. To face life parentless we can only imagine
what the future might hold for her. Like the fairy tale, "The Little Orphan Girl," the child is alone; we do not know the parental messages she
has to hold or the ancestral heritage that must be carried. We only know
she will face a life without the containment, and yet there is a life to be
lived and a destiny to be fulfilled.

---

224   von Franz, *The Cat*, p. 86.
225   von Franz, *The Cat*, p. 87.

Figure 20. Bellerophon Fights the Chimaera by Bernard Picart.
Source: Bridgeman Art Library. Reprinted by permission.

In the painting by Bernard Picart, "Bellerophon Fights the Chimaera," one sees the intense fight that must go on with the dark and sinister
(Figure 20). Chimaera was a fire-spewing monster in Greek mythology,

often depicted with the head of a lion, a body of a goat, and a tail of a dragon or snake. This composite creature devastated his surroundings until Bellerophon killed him. Bellerophon is riding Pegasus, a winged horse, which sprang from Medusa when Perseus cut off her head.[226] Later Pegasus became a symbol of intelligence, especially poetic, creativity.[227] Interestingly, Bellerophon, a Greek hero, was forced to leave his parents' court and when he refused the advances of King Proetus's wife, Stheneboea, she told her husband Bellerophon had tried to seduce her. Since the King did not question his wife, he sent Bellerophon to his father-in-law, instructing him to kill him. Bellerophon was then set to various tasks in the hopes he would meet his death, but he survived all these trials, even destroying the Chimaera.[228] The point of our story of the orphan is that we do have trials to face not because we are bad, but because life circumstances present themselves, and they are dark and sinister and life threatening, not only to our physical but also to our emotional existence. This painting illustrates the need for contact with the instincts and the spiritual realm to become more differentiated.

Wladislaw Slewinski has drawn "Orphan in Poronin," which so clearly depicts the feeling of being abandoned and alone (Figure 21). He is in black, suggesting the alchemical stage of the *nigredo*. The *nigredo* is the beginning of the suffering, the darkness of the soul, and often referred to as the "night sea journey" by Jung.[229] It is a time of looking at the things which were not seen before, the shadow. But more than this, it is connected with the dark aspect of the self as symbolized by the black hat. In the Middle Ages hat, *huot* in Old High German[230] meant that God's protection is with me.[231] This time of suffering is great and it is the Great Mother that gives and takes life and so it is with a great deal of suffering we meet the dark side of her. It is not just a personal suffering, but also the suffering of the dark side of God. This is facing oneself in all one's nakedness.

---

226 E. Burr, *The Chiron Dictionary of Greek and Roman Mythology*.

227 *The Herder Dictionary of Symbols*.

228 *The Herder Dictionary of Symbols*.

229 Jung, Symbols of the Mother and of Rebirth, *Symbols*, CW 5, ¶ 308.

230 E. Partridge, *Origins: A Short Etymological Dictionary of Modern Language*.

231 Schweizer, personal communication, February 28, 2001.

Figure 21. Orphan in Poronin by Wladislaw Slewinski. Source:
Muzeum Narodowe w Warszawie (The National Museum of
Warsaw, Poland). Reprinted by permission.

Figure 22. A Rest by the Way by Thomas Faed. Source: The
Bridgeman Art Library. Reprinted by permission.

To continue with the alchemical symbolism, the next painting by Thomas Faed, "A Rest on the Way," illustrates the *albedo* (Figure 22). There is still suffering but some quiet, lightening up of the process. At this stage we begin to acquire discriminating ability and some perspective on what has been occurring. The work is still progressing, but we can achieve some distance from the chaos. The painting shows a weary child on the journey and the light in the sky suggests there is hope and a future.

Figure 23. The Orphan of the Temple by Edward Matthew Ward.
Source: The Bridgeman Art Library. Reprinted by permission.

In the last painting by Edward Matthew Ward, entitled "The Orphan of the Temple," we see a young woman drawing as she sits before the temple (Figure 23). Here is the *rubedo*, a coming to the essence of a truth for oneself through the suffering. We see her drawing, suggesting that she is now in contact with the Self so that there is creative expression. The woman behind her seems to be a positive shadow figure looking over her shoulder approvingly. The man in the background appears as a potential animus figure, and he has to wait until she is finished with what she has to do. The dog sits close by, watching and seemingly very connected to her on the instinctual level. The goat in the foreground also watches and seems to represent the *prima materia*, an embodiment of the primal mother since she is an orphan. This connection to an archetypal versus a personal mother allows her to feel held and contained in the sense she is free to be all that she can be. Von Franz[232] refers to a state of psychological balance where there is no goats' blood and where sensuality does not sweep away the personality. She is all alone and yet she is now at one with herself, connected with her creativity, and her instincts and she is capable of distinguishing the true from the false. Here one can see the ego no longer as master, the Self can now express itself in an authentic way unique to her.

This painting illustrates a certain strength. It is not the active masculine strength of fighting a dragon, but a passive strength that comes out of the suffering. It is a feminine strength that comes out of trusting nature and trusting the great goddess. She need not act, but be patient and wait. It takes "a tremendous strength not to act."[233] In our present patriarchal society where the pressure is doing something and solving a problem quickly, it is an act of courage to wait. This does not mean we are only passive, but that we must understand all the things the unconscious produces during a particular conflict. Jung stated, "There is nothing I can do except wait, with a certain trust in God, until, out of a conflict borne with patience and fortitude, there emerges the solution destined—although I cannot see it—for that particular person."[234]

---

232 von Franz, *Alchemy.*
233 Schweizer, personal communication, February 28, 2001.
234 Jung, Introduction to the Religious and Psychological Problems of Alchemy, *Psychology and Alchemy, CW 12,* ¶ 37.

This feeling of being an orphan comes out of a sense of abandonment and seems to be a specific condition where the person is left feeling all alone in the world. The treatment for such a wounding has to do with seeing an unfolding process within the context of a development gone awry. This involves a kind of re-parenting and being with the analysand in a way that allows for that reconnection to the inner genuine self. This is about accompanying the individual who feels alone at whatever stage in life he or she may be, and it is about using all we know to affectively attune to them. The person, who feels orphaned, feels all alone and yet may have had a very good family that did not know how or could not emotionally be present. As analysts, this is not an easy task because we have to face our own fears of intimacy, narcissistic needs, and of being close in order to be with the other. Moreover, one is helping the individual to experience the necessary support and validation so that consciousness can be increased in the process of an individuation that is guided by the Self.

Concluding Remarks

In the setting of the lake and the mountains at Bollingen, Jung's stone set the initial context from which to explore the orphan. The stone is an orphan and Jung's carving from alchemical sayings, *Orphanus sum*, I am an orphan, was fitting. The orphan evokes many images, but most of all it is an archetype for being all alone in the world. This archetype can be evoked from being literally orphaned, parentless, to being on the journey toward wholeness or individuation. The path of individuation must be embarked upon alone, but paradoxically it also must be done in relationship to an Other.

To be an orphan is not so much about separation, loss, or abandonment, but about a meaning that is developed in the context in which it happens. It can be an early emotional abandonment, yet developmentally this is about a relationship gone awry, specifically of not experiencing a secure enough base. From the studies of the importance of having parents, there has been a movement toward foster instead of orphanage placements of children at least in the United States of America. The premise being that if there are parents in the home, there is the potential for bonding and feeling as if one belonged to someone. But the feeling of being an orphan can be present even when there are parents in the home because the orphan archetype has been activated. Certainly we need to become more conscious about relationships, but avoiding the orphan within us is not the answer. When we can embrace who we are with all our feelings of being alone in the world, then we can be generative toward and with others.

The attachment literature was acknowledged because the early relationships that is formed and out of which we seek to foster our uniqueness as an individual is important. Jung referenced this when he spoke about the place and the setting of the orphan stone. These early relationships help to organize and regulate human behavior and experience, on the one hand, and on the other hand, the archetypes are interwoven with these environmental influences including the temperament of the infant and the reaction from the caregivers. Depending on the circumstances, this may lead to the origin of many complexes including the orphan complex. Often times, the uniqueness of the individual goes unseen, and when this happens the connection to one's creativity is hampered; there may be problems with unrealistic expectations that others have for us, of missed opportunities for relating as relationships are fraught with projections.

While these early personal relationships are very important, not because they need to be perfect, but because they are opportunities for being seen and heard and validated for being in the world, they do not tell the whole story. A baby is no less than a miracle and it holds the hope for the future, and the child is the symbol for the potential for wholeness in each of us so we must look beyond the personal realm and into the symbolic realm. Frequently dreams provide a key. In addition, the metaphor of the baby being held and attended to is a reconnecting to the mother archetype that is so important for the orphan to gain a sense of containment and holding in order to go forth in the world.

The ability to be alone in the world is fostered by early relationships and, as Winnicott[235] explained, develops during the experience of being

---

235 D. W. Winnicott, *The Maturational Processes and the Facilitating Environment: Studies in the Theory of Emotional Development.*

alone in the presence of another. This physical and emotional presence, yet separation, allows the child to stay in connection with his own uniqueness. At the archetypal level we also must reconcile with our individual aloneness. The orphan appears prominent in our society today, as a correction to the logos one-sidedness. That is, the prominence of these orphans calls us to be more conscious of the importance of relating and connecting with others. In addition, we are at a time with current child-rearing practices, which suggests a parentless world, where the child sets the tone for what is needed from the parents. In actuality, there is more need for containment, relationship, relating, and Eros.

The child signifies the potential of approaching wholeness; that is, something evolving toward independence. While the orphan may emerge from a story of abandonment, exposure, and danger, these are all elaborations of its mysterious and miraculous birth and the object is the emergence of a new and unknown content.[236] The unknown content is a creative act that requires holding the tension of the opposites whereby the numinous or creative experience may unfold signifying a higher stage of self-realization. Then we may be in touch with our nature, instincts, and power; and here it represents the divine child and "…a personification of vital forces quite outside the limited range of our conscious mind."[237] On a symbolic level the child without parents indicates a content of the unconscious that is far removed or unrelated to the consciousness of our time. The effect is the potential to enlarge consciousness, to overcome an earlier unconscious state. We seem to be fascinated with the orphan who corrects a too one-sided attitude. The orphan as an archetype stirs up feelings and this is what is needed in relationships today. It is paradoxical to think that being an orphan, alone, would stimulate feelings to relate.

For the orphan necessitates an individuation journey as we saw in the fairy tale, "The Little Orphan Girl." This is a call to be the best we can be and to come to our own true nature. However, the development of this higher consciousness is equivalent to being *all alone in the world*. This being alone in the world does not mean one is lonely, but it does

236 Jung, Child Archetype, *Archetypes, CW 9i*, ¶ 285.
237 Jung, Child Archetype, *Archetypes, CW 9i*, ¶ 289.

mean reconnecting to something infinite so that we can be alone yet at one with the world.

The orphan suffers an existential bereavement or yearning and religion or some form of spirituality offers a way out. That is, it offers a healing through hope that there is some reason for this happening in my life. It is part of my story and hence I am alone, but not left alone for there is hope that my life will have importance not because I have survived but because I have learned to thrive despite these experiences. In many cases, this means growing an internal mother who knows how to take care of me and be good to me. This new attitude needs intuition, common sense, and consciousness that know about the good and bad parts about my history and myself and then using them as a guide. Once one can experience the opposites, then the possibility of an accommodation with the unconscious may lead to a synthesis of conscious and unconscious knowledge and action. The orphan is typically very alert because she is so intuitive, but she will override her intuition if she thinks another will love her and this may distract her from the individual path.

The journey of the orphan is to become in touch with all that he or she can be. To become in touch with the creativity that exists within all of us to become whole. This combined with self-reflection reestablishes hope and a sense that I have a future. There is a thread of life, a sense of belonging, a sense of future and continuity. The child or adult who feels abandoned and not seen by activation of the archetype is an orphan, but *orphanus sum* means I am an orphan and I own, that is take responsibility for, my own story. It is a privileged journey in which one can at some point in time say with pride, I am an orphan.

BIBLIOGRAPHY

Aarne, A. *The Types of Folktale* (2nd rev.). (S. Thompson, Trans.). Helsinki, Finland: Academia Scientiarum Fennica, 1987.

Abram, J. *The Language of Winnicott: A Dictionary and Guide to Understanding His Work*. Northvale, NJ: Aronson, 1996.

Abt, T. *Introduction to Picture Interpretation: According to C.G. Jung*. Zurich, Switzerland: Living Human Heritage Publications, 2005.

Adler, G. & Jaffe, A. (Eds.). (R.F.C. Hull trans.). *C.G. Jung Letters, Volume 2*. Princeton, NJ: Princeton University Press, 1975.

Ainsworth, M.D.S. *Infancy in Uganda: Infant Care and the Growth of Love*. Baltimore, MD: Johns Hopkins University Press, 1967.

Ainsworth, M.D.S., Blehar, M.C., Waters, E., & Wall, S. *Patterns of Attachment: A Psychological Study of the Strange Situation*. Hillsdale, NJ: Erlbaum, 1978.

Allen, R.E. (Ed.). *The Concise Oxford Dictionary of Current English*. Oxford, England: Clarendon Press, 1990.

Asper, K. *The Abandoned Child Within: On Losing and Regaining Self-Worth* (S.E. Rooks, Trans.). New York, NY: Fromm, 1987.

Awdry, W. *Thomas, the Tank Engine*. London, England: Heinemann Young Books, 1998.

Becker, U. (Ed.). *The Element Encyclopedia of Symbols*. Shafesbury, Dorset, England: Element, 1994.

Beebe, B. & Lachmann, F.M. *Infant Research and Adult Treatment: Co-Constructing Interactions*. Hillsdale, NJ: The Analytic Press, 2002.

Bowlby, J. Grief and Mourning in Infancy and Early Childhood. *The Psychoanalytic Study of the Child*, 15, 9-52, 1960.

——— *Child Care and the Growth of Love*. London, England: Penguin Books, 1965.

——— *Attachment and Loss. Vol. III: Loss, Sadness, and Depression*. New York, NY: Basic Books, 1980.

——— *Attachment and Loss. Vol. I: Attachment* (2nd ed.). New York, NY: Basic Books, 1982.

Briggs, K. *A Dictionary of British Folk-Tales in the English Language, Part A* (Vol. 1). London, England: Routledge & Kegan Paul, 1970.

Brown, F., Driver, S.R., & Briggs, C.A. *Hebrew and English Lexicon of the Old Testament*. London, England: Oxford University Press, 1907.

Bulfinch, T. *Bulfinch's Mythology*. New York, NY: HarperCollins Publishers, 1991.

Burr, E. (Trans.). *The Chiron Dictionary of Greek and Roman Mythology*. Wilmette, IL: Chiron, 1994.

Chun, N. Faces of the Abandoned. *Newsweek*. http://www.newsweek. com/2007/12/12/faces-of-the-abondoned.html, 2007

Cleary, T. (Trans. & Ed.). *Immortal Sisters: Secret Teachings of Taoist Women*. Berkeley, CA: North Atlantic Books, 1996.

———— (Trans.). *The Taoist Classics, Volume 3*. Boston, MA: Shambhala, 2003.

Costantino, M. *Georgia O'Keefe*. Greenwich, CT: Brompton Books, Corp, 1994.

De Mause, L. (Ed.). *The History of Childhood*. New York, NY: The Psychohistory Press, 1974.

De Vries, A. *Dictionary of Symbols and Imagery*. Amsterdam, Holland: North-Holland Publishing Company, 1974.

Dickens, C. *Oliver Twist*. The Anniversary Edition of the Works of Charles Dickens, February 7, 1812. New York, NY: P F Collier & Son, 1911.

Douglas, C. (Ed.). *Visions: Notes of the Seminar Given in 1930-1934 by C.G. Jung*. Princeton, NJ: Princeton University Press, 1997.

Edinger, E.F. *The Bible and the Psyche: Individuation Symbolism in the Old Testament*. Toronto, Canada: Inner City Books, 1986.

———— *Ego and Archetype*. Boston, MA: Shambhala, 1992.

———— *The Aion Lectures: Exploring the Self in C.G. Jung's Aion*. Toronto, Canada: Inner City Books, 1996.

Emde, R.N. The Pre-Representational Self and Its Affective Core. *Psychoanalytic Study of the Child*, 1983; 38: 165-192.

———— Development Terminable and Interminable. I. Innate and Motivational Factors from Infancy. *International Journal of Psychoanalysis*, 1988; 69: 23-42.

Estes, C.P. *Women Who Run With the Wolves: Myths and Stories of the Wild Woman Archetype*. New York, NY: Ballantine Books, 1992.

Evans, R.I. *Conversations With Carl Jung and Reactions from Ernest Jones*. Princeton, NJ: D. Van Nostrand Company, Inc., 1964.

Evetts-Secker, J. *Orphanos Exoikos: The Precarious Possibility of Wholeness* (The Guild of Pastoral Psychology, Guild Lecture 272). Middlesex, England: Abacus Print, 2000.

Grynbaum, G.A. The Secrets of Harry Potter. *The San Francisco Jung Institute Library Journal*, 2001; 19 (4): pp. 17-48.

Hastings, J. (Ed.). *A Dictionary of the Bible (Vol. 3)*. New York, NY: Scribner's Sons, 1909.

Henderson, J.L. *Cultural Attitudes in Psychological Perspective*. Toronto, Canada: Inner City Books, 1984.

Hilditch, T. Chinese Cultural Studies: A Holocaust of Little Girls. *South China Morning Post* in World Press Review, 1995; September: p. 39.

Hill, J. *The Tristan Legend: A Confrontation Between Logos and Eros*. Unpublished thesis, C.G. Jung Institute, Zurich, Switzerland, 1972.

Holmes, J. *John Bowlby and Attachment Theory*. London, England: Routledge, 1993.

Hsu, J. There Are More Boys Than Girls in China and India: Preference for Sons Could Spell Trouble for China and India. *Scientific American*, 2008: August 4. http://www.scientificamerican.com/article.cfm?id=there-are-more-boys-than-girls

Jacobi, J. *Complex/Archetype/Symbol in the Psychology of C.G. Jung* (R. Manheim, Trans.). New York: Princeton University Press, 1959.

Jacoby, M. *Jungian Psychotherapy and Contemporary Modern Infant Research: Basic Patterns of Emotional Exchange* (R. Weathers, Trans.). London, England: Routledge, 1999.

Jaffe, A. (Ed.). *Word and Image*. Princeton, NJ: Princeton University Press, 1979.

Jobes, G. *Dictionary of Mythology Folklore and Symbols, Part 2*. New York, NY: The Scarecrow Press, 1962.

Jung, C.G. *The Collected Works, Second Edition*. (Bollingen Series XX; H. Read, M. Fordham, & G. Adler, Eds.; R. F. C. Hull, Trans.). Princeton, NJ: Princeton University Press, 1953-1979.

————— *Aion: Researches into the Phenomenology of the Self, The Collected Works Vol. 9ii, Second Edition.* (Bollingen Series XX). Princeton, NJ: Princeton University Press, 1969.

————— *Alchemical Studies, The Collected Works Vol. 13, Second Edition.* (Bollingen Series XX). Princeton, NJ: Princeton University Press, 1968.

————— *Children's Dreams: Notes from the Seminar Given in 1936-1940 by C.G. Jung.* Princeton, NJ: Princeton University Press, 2008.

————— *Memories, Dreams, Reflections* (A. Jaffe, Ed.; R. & C. Winston, Trans.). London, England: Collins & Routledge & Kegan Paul, 1963.

————— *Mysterium Coniunctionis, The Collected Works Vol. 14, Second Edition.* (Bollingen Series XX). Princeton, NJ: Princeton University Press, 1970.

————— *Psychological Types, The Collected Works Vol. 6, Second Edition.* (Bollingen Series XX). Princeton, NJ: Princeton University Press, 1971.

————— *Psychology and Alchemy, The Collected Works Vol. 12, Second Edition.* (Bollingen Series XX). Princeton, NJ: Princeton University Press, 1968.

————— *Psychology and Religion, The Collected Works Vol. 11, Second Edition.* (Bollingen Series XX). Princeton, NJ: Princeton University Press, 1970.

————— *Symbols of Transformation, The Collected Works Vol. 5, Second Edition.* (Bollingen Series XX). Princeton, NJ: Princeton University Press, 1967.

————— *Two Essays on Analytical Psychology, The Collected Works Vol. 7, Second Edition.* (Bollingen Series XX). Princeton, NJ: Princeton University Press, 1967.

————— *The Archetypes and the Collective Unconscious, The Collected Works Vol. 9i, Second Edition.* (Bollingen Series XX). Princeton, NJ: Princeton University Press, 1969.

————— *The Practice of Psychotherapy, The Collected Works Vol. 16, Second Edition.* (Bollingen Series XX). Princeton, NJ: Princeton University Press, 1966.

———— *The Red Book: Liber Novus.* (S. Shamdasani, Ed.; M. Kyburz, J. Peck, S. Shamdasani, Trans.). New York, NY: W.W. Norton & Company, 2009.

———— *The Structure and Dynamics of the Psyche, The Collected Works Vol. 8, Second Edition.* (Bollingen Series XX). Princeton, NJ: Princeton University Press, 1969.

Jung, C.G., von Franz, M-L., Henderson, J.L., Jacobi, J., & Jaffe, A. *Man and His Symbols.* Garden City, NY: Doubleday & Company, Inc, 1964.

Karen, R. *Becoming Attached: First Relationships and How They Shape Our Capacity to Love.* New York, NY: Oxford University Press, 1998.

Kerenyi, C. *The Gods of the Greeks.* London, England: Thames & Hudson, 1961.

———— The Primordial Child in Primordial Times. In C.G. Jung & C. Kerenyi, *Essays on a Science of Mythology: The Myth of the Divine Child and the Mysteries of Eleusis* (R.F.C. Hull, Trans.). Princeton, NJ: Princeton University Press, 1993.

Klaus, M.H., & Kennell, J.H. *Parent-Infant Bonding* (2nd ed.). St. Louis, MO: Mosby, 1982.

Klein, E. *A Comprehensive Etymological Dictionary of the English Language, Unabridged, One-Volume Edition.* Elsevier: Amsterdam, Netherlands, 1971.

Kohut, H. *The Analysis of the Self: A Systematic Approach to the Psychoanalytic Treatment of Narcissistic Personality Disorders.* New York, NY: International Universities Press, 1971.

Korczak, J. (n.d.). http://en.wikipedia.org/wiki/Janusz_Korczak/ Retrieved May 29, 2011.

Lacinius, J. *Pretiosa Margarita Novella de Thesauro ac Pretiosissimo Philosophorum Lapide.* Venedig: Aldus, 1546.

Lichtenberg, J.D. *Psychoanalysis and Motivation.* Hillsdale, NJ: The Analytic Press, 1989.

Magnuson, J., & Petrie, D.G. *Orphan Train.* New York, NY: The Dial Press, 1978.

Main, M., Kaplan, N. & Cassidy, I. Security, Infancy, Childhood and Adulthood: A Move to the Level of Representation. In J. Bretherton & E. Waters (Eds.). *Monographs of the Society for Research in Child Development,* 1985; 50, (1-2) Serial No. 209: pp. 64-104.

Matthews, Boris. (Trans.) *The Herder Dictionary of Symbols*. Wilmette, IL: Chiron, 1993.

Merton, T. *The Collected Poems of Thomas Merton*. New York, NY: New Directions Publishing Company, 1977.

Miller, B. (Trans.). *The Bhagavad-Gita*. New York, NY: Bantam Books, 1986.

Mitchell, R.R. & Friedman, H.S. *Sandplay: Past, Present and Future*. New York, NY: Routledge, 1994.

Muhammad: Legacy of a Prophet, 2002. http://www.pbs.org/muhammad/timeline_html.shtml Retrieved April 29, 2012.

Nelson, P. *There's a Hole in My Sidewalk: The Romance of Self-Discovery*. New York, NY: Atria Books, 2012.

Nouwen, H.J.M. *The Wounded Healer*. New York, NY: Image Books Doubleday, 1972.

Oakes, M. *The Stone Speaks: The Memoir of a Personal Transformation*. Wilmette, IL: Chiron, 1987.

Paredes, A. *Folktales of Mexico*. Chicago, IL: The University of Chicago Press, 1970.

Partridge, E. *Origins: A Short Etymological Dictionary of Modern Language* (3rd ed.). London, England: Routledge & Kegan Paul, 1961.

Pino-Saavedra, Y. (Ed.) *Folktales of Chile*. Chicago, IL: The University of Chicago Press, 1967.

Punnett, A.F. Symptom, Symbol and Sandplay: Manifestation of a Tic Disorder in a Child. *Journal of Sandplay Therapy*, 2009; 18, (1): 27-45.

Rank, O. The Myth of the Birth of the Hero. In R. A. Segal (Eds.), *In Quest of the Hero* (pp. 30-86). Princeton, NJ: Princeton University Press, 1990.

Rinchen, G.S. *The Thirty-Seven Practices of Bodhisattvas*. (R. Sonam, Ed. & Trans.). Ithaca, NY: Snow Lion Publications, 1997.

Ronnberg, A. & Martin, K. (Eds.). *The Book of Symbols*. Cologne, Germany: Taschen, 2010.

Rumi, J. (C. Barks, Trans.). *The Essential Rumi*. San Francisco, CA: HarperCollins, 1995.

Schore, A.N. *Affect Regulation and the Origin of the Self: The Neurobiology of Emotional Development*. Hillsdale, NJ: Erlbaum, 1994.

—— The Experience-Dependent Maturation of a Regulatory System in the Orbital Prefrontal Cortex and the Origin of Developmental Psychopathology. *Development and Psychopathology*, 1996; 8: 59-87.

—— A Century After Freud's Project: Is a Rapprochement Between Psychoanalysis and Neurobiology at Hand. *Journal of American Psychoanalytic Association*, 1997a; 45: 841-867.

—— Early Organization of the Nonlinear Right Brain and Development of a Predisposition to Psychiatric Disorders. *Development and Psychopathology*, 1997b; 9: 595-631.

—— *Affect Regulation and the Repair of the Self*. New York, NY: W.W. Norton & Company, 2003.

Schweizer, A. *The Sungod's Journey Through the Netherworld: Reading the Ancient Egyptian Amudat*. Ithaca, NY & London, England: Cornell University Press, 2010.

Sidoli, M & Davies, M. *Jungian Child Psychotherapy: Individuation in Childhood*. London, England: Karnac Books, 1988.

Simpson, D.P. *Cassell's Latin Dictionary*. London, England: Cassell, 1979.

Simpson, E. *Orphans: Real and Imaginary*. New York, NY: Weidenfeld & Nicolson, 1987.

Singer, T. & Kimbles, S.L. (Eds.) *The Cultural Complex: Contemporary Jungian Perspectives on Psyche and Society*. Hove, England & New York, NY: Brunner-Routledge, 2004.

Spiegelman, J.M. & Miyuki, M. *Buddhism and Jungian Psychology*. Tempe, AZ: New Falcon Publications, 1994.

Sroufe, L.A. Relationships, Self, and Individual Adaptation. In A.J. Sameroff & R.N. Emde (Eds.), *Relationship Disturbances in Early Childhood*. New York, NY: Basic Books, 1989.

Stern, D.N. *The Interpersonal World of the Infant*. New York, NY: Basic Books, 1985.

—— *The Motherhood Constellation*. New York, NY: Basic Books, 1995.

Suzuki, D.T. *Essays in Zen Buddhism*. New York, NY: Grove Press, 1949.

The Interpreter's Dictionary of the Bible (Vol. 2.). New York, NY: Abdington Press, 1962.

The New Encyclopedia Britannica. (Vol. 4, 15th ed.). Chicago, IL: Encyclopedia Britannica, 1985.

Thompson, S. *One Hundred Favorite Folktales*. Bloomington, IN: Indiana University Press, 1968.

———— *The Folktale*. New York, NY: AMS Press, 1979. (Original work 1946).

Thoreau, H.D. *Walden or Life in the Woods*. Boston, MA: Houghton Mifflin Company, 1910.

Thurston, A.F. In a Chinese Orphanage. *The Atlantic Monthly*, 1996; 277, 4: pp. 28-43.

Trevarthen, C. The Self Born in Intersubjectivity: The Psychology of an Infant Communicating. In U. Neisser (Ed.), *The Perceived Self: Ecological and Interpersonal Sources of Self-Knowledge*. New York, NY: Cambridge University Press, 1993.

von Franz, M-L. *Number and Time: Reflections Leading Toward Unification of Depth Psychology and Physics* (A. Dykes, Trans.). Evanston, IL: Northwestern University Press, 1974.

———— *Alchemy: An Introduction to the Symbolism and the Psychology*. Toronto, Canada: Inner City Books, 1980.

———— *The Feminine in Fairy Tales* (rev. ed.). Boston, MA: Shambhala, 1993.

———— *Interpretation of Fairy Tales* (rev. ed.). Boston, MA & London: Shambhala, 1996.

———— *Archetypal Dimensions of the Psyche*. Boston, MA: Shambhala, 1997.

———— *The Cat: A Tale of Feminine Redemption*. Toronto, Canada: Inner City Books, 1999.

Wada, S. (G.P. Sakamoto, Trans.). *The Oxherder: A Zen Parable Illustrated*. New York, NY: George Braziller, 2002.

Wilhelm, R. (Trans.) *I Ching*, Second Edition. Princeton, NJ: Princeton University Press, 1961.

Winnicott, D.W. *The Maturational Processes and the Facilitating Environment: Studies in the Theory of Emotional Development*. New York, NY: International Universities Press, 1965.

Wright, K. *Vision and Separation: Between Mother and Baby*. Northvale, NJ: Aronson, 1991.

Zeanah, C.H., Jr. & Boris, N.W. Disturbances and Disorders of Attachment in Early Childhood. In C.H. Zeanah, Jr. (Ed.), *Handbook of Infant Mental Health* (2nd ed., pp. 353-368). New York, NY: The Guilford Press, 2000.

PERMISSIONS

Many thanks to all who have directly or indirectly provided permission to quote their works, including:

Bridgeman Art Library. Reprinted by Permission of Bridgeman Art Library.

"Cana" by Thomas Merton, from The Collected Poems of Thomas Merton, copyright© 1946 by New Directions Publishing Corporation, 1977 by The Trustees of the Merton Legacy Trust. Reprinted by permission of New Directions Publishing Corp.

From The Zen Ox-herder. Translation by Gen. P. Sakomoto. Illustrated by Stephanie Wada. Copyright ©2002 by George Braziller. New York, NY. George Braziller, Inc. Used by permission of George Braziller, Inc. All rights reserved.

'Frozen Out' Reprinted by Permission of Bridgeman Art Library & Mabel Lucie Attwell © Lucie Attwell Ltd.

Getty Images. Reprinted by Permission of Getty Images.

The Collected Works of C.G. Jung, C.G. Jung's Word and Image. All per PUP editions. Reprinted by permission of Princeton University Press.

The Collected Works of C.G. Jung, Vol. 13 ©1967 Princeton University Press. 1996 renewed PUP. Reprinted by permission of Princeton University Press.

"Orphan in Poronin" by Slewinski Reprinted by permission of Muzeum Narodowe w Warszawie (The National Museum of Warsaw, Poland).

Fairy Tale, The Little Orphan Girl. Reprinted by permission of University of Chicago Press.

Poem by Sun Bu-er from Immortal Sisters: Secret Teachings of Taoist Women translated and edited by Thomas Cleary, published by North Atlantic Books, copyright ©1989, 1996 by Thomas Cleary. Reprinted by permission of publisher.

"The Guest House" by J. Rumi. Translation by Coleman Barks. Copyright ©1995 by Coleman Barks. Used by permission of Coleman Barks. All rights reserved.

"Autobiography in 5 Chapters" reprinted with the permission of Beyond Words/Atria Publishing Group from *There's a Hole in my Sidewalk: The Romance of Self-discovery* by Portia Nelson. Copyright © 1993 by Portia Nelson. All rights reserved.

INDEX

Y

yang 61, 65, 128
yin 61, 65, 128

Z

Zeus 16, 77, 84

ABOUT THE AUTHOR

Audrey F. Punnett, Ph.D., is a graduate of the C.G. Jung Institute, Zurich with diplomas in both Child/Adolescent and Adult Analytical Psychology. She is an Associate Clinical Professor, Psychiatry, the University of California San Francisco – Fresno; Adjunct Professor, Alliant International University; Registered Play Therapist – Supervisor, and Certified Sandplay Therapist – Teacher, ISST & STA, past President of the Board of Trustees. She is a member of AGAP, serving on the Board, and the CGJI-SF, past Chair of the Infant, Child & Adolescent Training Committee (iCAT). She has lectured and given workshops on the orphan in Europe, New Zealand, Taiwan, Canada and the USA, and published in peer reviewed Journals. Dr. Punnett maintains a private practice in Fresno, California.

You might also enjoy reading:

Marked By Fire: Stories of the Jungian Way edited by Patricia Damery &
Naomi Ruth Lowinsky, 1ˢᵗ Ed., Trade Paperback, 180pp, Biblio., 2012
— ISBN 978-1-926715-68-1

The Dream and Its Amplification edited by Erel Shalit & Nancy Swift
Furlotti, 1ˢᵗ Ed., Trade Paperback, 180pp, Biblio., 2013
— ISBN 978-1-926715-89-6

Shared Realities: Participation Mystique and Beyond edited by Mark
Windborn, 1ˢᵗ Ed., Trade Paperback, 270pp, Index, Biblio., 2014
— ISBN 978-1-77169-009-6

Pierre Teilhard de Chardin and C.G. Jung: Side by Side edited by Fred
Gustafson, 1ˢᵗ Ed., Trade Paperback, 270pp, Index, Biblio., 2014
— ISBN 978-1-77169-014-0

Re-Imagining Mary: A Journey Through Art to the Feminine Self
by Mariann Burke, 1ˢᵗ Ed., Trade Paperback, 180pp, Index, Biblio., 2009
— ISBN 978-0-9810344-1-6

Advent and Psychic Birth
by Mariann Burke, Revised Ed., Trade Paperback, 170pp, 2014
— ISBN 978-1-926715-99-5

Transforming Body and Soul
by Steven Galipeau, Rev. Ed., Trade Paperback, 180pp, Index, Biblio., 2011
— ISBN 978-1-926715-62-9

Lifting the Veil: Revealing the Other Side by Fred Gustafson & Jane
Kamerling, 1ˢᵗ Ed, Paperback, 170pp, Biblio., 2012
— ISBN 978-1-926715-75-9

Resurrecting the Unicorn: Masculinity in the 21ˢᵗ Century
by Bud Harris, Rev. Ed., Trade Paperback, 300pp, Index, Biblio., 2009
— ISBN 978-0-9810344-0-9

The Father Quest: Rediscovering an Elemental Force
by Bud Harris, Reprint, Trade Paperback, 180pp, Index, Biblio., 2009
— ISBN 978-0-9810344-9-2

Like Gold Through Fire: The Transforming Power of Suffering
by Massimilla & Bud Harris, Reprint, Trade Paperback, 150pp, Index,
Biblio., 2009 — ISBN 978-0-9810344-5-4

The Art of Love: The Craft of Relationship by Massimilla and Bud Harris,
1st Ed. Trade Paperback, 150pp, 2010
— ISBN 978-1-926715-02-5

Divine Madness: Archetypes of Romantic Love by John R. Haule, Rev. Ed.,
Trade Paperback, 282pp, Index, Biblio., 2010
— ISBN 978-1-926715-04-9

Tantra and Erotic Trance in 2 volumes by John R. Haule
  Volume 1 - Outer Work, 1st Ed. Trade Paperback, 215pp, Index,
  Bibliograpy, 2012 — ISBN 978-0-9776076-8-6
  Volume 2 - Inner Work, 1st Ed. Trade Paperback, 215pp, Index,
  Bibliograpy, 2012 — ISBN 978-0-9776076-9-3

Eros and the Shattering Gaze: Transcending Narcissism
by Ken Kimmel, 1st Ed., Trade Paperback, 310pp, Index, Biblio., 2011
— ISBN 978-1-926715-49-0

The Sister From Below: When the Muse Gets Her Way
by Naomi Ruth Lowinsky, 1st Ed., Trade Paperback, 248pp, Index, Biblio.,
2009 — ISBN 978-0-9810344-2-3

The Motherline: Every Woman's Journey to find her Female Roots
by Naomi Ruth Lowinsky, Reprint, Trade Paperback, 252pp, Index, Biblio.,
2009 — ISBN 978-0-9810344-6-1

The Dairy Farmer's Guide to the Universe in 4 volumes
by Dennis L. Merritt:
  Volume 1 - Jung and Ecopsychology, 1st Ed., Trade Paperback, 242pp,
  Index, Biblio., 2011 — ISBN 978-1-926715-42-1
  Volume 2 - The Cry of Merlin: Jung the Prototypical Ecopsychologist, 1st
  Ed., Trade Paperback, 204pp, Index, Biblio., 2012
  — ISBN 978-1-926715-43-8
  Volume 3 - Hermes, Ecopsychology, and Complexity Theory,
  1st Ed., Trade Paperback, 228pp, Index, Biblio., 2012
  — ISBN 978-1-926715-44-5
  Volume 4 - Land, Weather, Seasons, Insects: An Archetypal View, 1st Ed.,
  Trade Paperback, 134pp, Index, Biblio., 2012
  — ISBN 978-1-926715-45-2

Four Eternal Women: Toni Wolff Revisited—A Study In Opposites
by Mary Dian Molton & Lucy Anne Sikes, 1st Ed., 320pp, Index, Biblio.,
2011 — ISBN 978-1-926715-31-5

Becoming: An Introduction to Jung's Concept of Individuation
by Deldon Anne McNeely, 1st Ed., Trade Paperback, 230pp, Index, Biblio.,
2010 — ISBN 978-1-926715-12-4

Animus Aeternus: Exploring the Inner Masculine by Deldon Anne
McNeely, Reprint, Trade Paperback, 196pp, Index, Biblio., 2011
— ISBN 978-1-926715-37-7

Mercury Rising: Women, Evil, and the Trickster Gods
by Deldon Anne McNeely, Revised, Trade Paperback, 200pp, Index, Biblio.,
2011 — ISBN 978-1-926715-54-4

Gathering the Light: A Jungian View of Meditation
by V. Walter Odajnyk, Revised Ed., Trade Paperback, 264pp, Index, Biblio.,
2011 — ISBN 978-1-926715-55-1

The Promiscuity Papers
by Matjaz Regovec, 1ˢᵗ Ed., Trade Paperback, 86pp, Index, Biblio., 2011
— ISBN 978-1-926715-38-4

Enemy, Cripple, Beggar: Shadows in the Hero's Path
by Erel Shalit, 1ˢᵗ Ed., Trade Paperback, 248pp, Index, Biblio., 2008
— ISBN 978-0-9776076-7-9

The Cycle of Life: Themes and Tales of the Journey
by Erel Shalit, 1ˢᵗ Ed., Trade Paperback, 210pp, Index, Biblio., 2011
— ISBN 978-1-926715-50-6

The Hero and His Shadow
by Erel Shalit, Revised Ed., Trade Paperback, 208pp, Index, Biblio., 2012
— ISBN 978-1-926715-69-8

Riting Myth, Mythic Writing: Plotting Your Personal Story
by Dennis Patrick Slattery, Trade Paperback, 220 pp. Biblio., 2012
— ISBN 978-1-926715-77-3

The Guilt Cure
by Nancy Carter Pennington & Lawrence H. Staples, 1ˢᵗ Ed., Trade
Paperback, 200pp, Index, Biblio., 2011 — ISBN 978-1-926715-53-7

Guilt with a Twist: The Promethean Way
by Lawrence Staples,1ˢᵗ Ed., Trade Paperback, 256pp, Index, Biblio., 2008
— ISBN 978-0-9776076-4-8

The Creative Soul: Art and the Quest for Wholeness
by Lawrence Staples, 1ˢᵗ Ed., Trade Paperback, 100pp, Index, Biblio., 2009
— ISBN 978-0-9810344-4-7

Deep Blues: Human Soundscapes for the Archetypal Journey
by Mark Winborn, 1ˢᵗ Ed., Trade Paperback, 130pp, Index, Biblio., 2011
— ISBN 978-1-926715-52-0

Phone Orders Welcomed
Credit Cards Accepted
In Canada & the U.S. call 1-800-228-9316
International call +1-831-238-7799
www.fisherkingpress.com

51601318R00100

Made in the USA
Lexington, KY
29 April 2016